TWO
WORLDS,
ONE
MIND

Lucille,
    thank you for
your support. ~~I~~ hope
my stories help your
work with others.
            Auxie

Two Worlds, One Mind

The Autobiography of an Autistic Woman-Child

Susan A. Shoemaker

To order additional copies of this book, contact:
Xlibris Corporation
1-888-795-4274
www.Xlibris.com
Orders@Xlibris.com
78352

CONTENTS

PREFACE

My name is Susie, and I have written this book to open hearts and minds into my world of Asperger's syndrome, a condition that falls in the autistic spectrum. It is my belief that the stories may prevent others who have Asperger's from being put into very vulnerable situations. Perhaps, if you know someone who has this disability, you can support them with positive daily safety nets.

This condition has been marked as a deficiency in social skills, transitions (or changes), and the insistence for sameness. We are literal, visual thinkers and, at times, are viewed as naïve, odd, socially clumsy, or eccentric, leading to teasing or bullying. We can have obsessive routines and may be preoccupied with a particular subject, idea, person, or activity.

As an Asperger's individual, I have a difficult time reading nonverbal cues (body language) or understanding the intentions of others, as well as an inability to process abstract thinking. Throughout my stories, you will see how comments and actions from others will spin my thoughts into a repeating frenzy until a trusted person can give a simple step or concrete direction of guidance to prevent floods of my anxiety from surfacing out of control. My rote memory has also been a tremendous benefit because this provides a mechanical, visual, hands-on way of doing something without thought.

My stories will take you on a journey into my world of music and play. For me, these "stuck-in-time" rituals are calming and necessary for my survival. And if there are no threatening elements close by, then my sensitivities to sounds, sights, and touch are reduced, allowing me to have a much more natural, spontaneous, and emotional relationship with others.

My story, to say the least, is about living in two worlds with one mind: the world of living with the affliction of Asperger's syndrome, and surviving in the real world where one does not experience life the same way.

It is my hope that, as the reader, you can connect the dots or make a solid connection into my life with Asperger's.

INTRODUCTION

A daughter born July 1962, Friday the thirteenth, at 5:55 AM, seven pounds, eight ounces, twenty-one inches. A blood transfusion was ordered due to the Rh factor. Different from the first two children born and the other four children who followed.

Many people had concerns regarding how I acted, responded, or thought. My memory of events goes way back—age two, to be exact: Recording words spoken by others along with very detailed picture memories and some actions of others. Struggling with words that have no picture to relate. Scrambled by others' emotions and unable to bond. Conflicts with new information, and a lack of understanding, and threatened by change.

At age sixteen, I was diagnosed with autism. My parents did not believe such nonsense. For that matter, they do not believe in psychiatry. Still, I went throughout my grown-up years going forward, backward, upside down, receiving diagnoses with no consistency until, at the age of thirty-nine, a remarkable chain of events sent me back full circle to who I am.

Perhaps my story can help people to realize that some things, you cannot fix or change, but rather, just accept that a natural learning order is most helpful.

"What Is Everyone Talking About?"

Throughout my forty-five years of life, many people (family, friends, teachers, neighbors, co-workers, bosses, professionals, or others)

have made verbal statements regarding how I act, respond, or think. Here is a wide variety of the most common among them:

"Susan, quit biting yourself!"

"Susan, stop banging your head on the floor!"

"Why are you hurting yourself?"

"Stop flapping your hands in the air—you look like a fairy!"

"Susan doesn't have any sense of pain."

"Put those shoulders down and stop rocking."

"Stop kicking your feet and carrying on this temper tantrum."

"Slow down!"

"Lift up your chin and look at me, not out in space."

"Stop screaming!"

"Stop yelling!"

"Talk slower!"

"You're too loud!"

"Stop your damn laughing; there is nothing funny about that."

"Susan is so sensitive about everything."

"Stop staring off somewhere and pay attention."

"Susan is nervous and jerky—mostly jerky."

"Are you deaf? Answer me."

"Your thinking is backwards."

"You are such a klutz."

"Why are you so clumsy?"

"What did you do now—crash?"

"Stop spinning that radio; you're going to break it!"

"Susan, will you stop spinning the dice and take your turn."

"Stop spinning the spinner; we want to play the game!"

"Stop, Susan, you're going to ruin the record player, turning the turntable by hand!"

"Sue, you talk about the same things over and over."

"Susie, we are tired of you asking us the same questions. We already answered it. No, the answer didn't change!"

"Susan, get out of that room and socialize!"

"Sue, why are you going on and on about the same thing? We are not even talking about that anymore."

"Susan is so damn stubborn."

"Why aren't you emotionally sensitive to other people?"
"Do you believe everything people say?"
"You take things people say way too literally!"
"You take things too seriously!"
"You have no sense of humor!"
"Nobody understands what the hell you are talking about!"
"What is wrong with you?"
"Susan, stop making that noise!"
"Susan, will you shut up!!!!"
"Listen to what I said—are you deaf?"
"You are a blockhead!"
"You are a half-wit!"
"Why do you do the same things all the time?"
"Why do you eat the same things all the time?"
"Don't talk to Susan. She won't understand!"
"Susan, we don't want to hear your problems!"
"Will you stop organizing everything!"
"You're weird!"
"You're odd!"
"You're stupid!"
"You're a retard!"
"Sue, you are so slow. You're not getting it!"
"You're always lost; that's why I love you!"
"God, you're so naive!"
"Gheez, you're a moron!"
"Stop talking with your hands and tell me what you want!"
"Close your mouth! You look like an idiot!"
"Stop pinching!"
"You are so exasperating!"
"You're crazy!"
"What is Susan so upset about?"
"Calm down!"
"You're a pain!"
"Stop pointing at things and speak up if you want something!"
"Well—Susan, we thought you were possessed!"
"You never did like change!"
"Susan, you are going to have to adjust to change in order to survive!"
"You are so task oriented."

"Do you do everything people tell you to do?"
"Susie, do you remember everything people say?"
"Susie, you have a remarkable memory!"
"You're like a computer!"
"You need to be yourself; you are a chronic people pleaser!"
"Don't touch her; she jumps!"

Comments like these or others would send an automatic wave of scrambling. The behaviors you want to change would become more intense, or an emotional outburst would follow. If you are displeased about us, then we are displeased with you but for different reasons. Ours are "Why?" "You don't make sense to me." "Your words hurt me." "Your actions hurt me." "Your tone of voice hurts me." "Your facial expression (if we can make eye contact) scares me." "Leave me alone!"

We may look at you with intense anger or wave our arms in a panicky motion. We may push things, kick, scream, bite, pinch, cry uncontrollably, or withdraw.

Physical contact becomes unbearable. Remember, we are scrambled. The words used by others cause friction in our brain circuits radiating throughout our body. Touching us amplifies the static.

We are visual processors and task oriented. Your actions are speaking louder than your words (with no picture to follow). Show us slowly with your actions (repeat this as many times as necessary), then ask us to do it that way. Our experiences have not yet developed like yours because we learn differently and are slower. Once we have a wide range of experience (which, of course, is the best teacher), then emotional times begin to develop (especially over time). Since we are this way, other teaching methods may include exaggerated sound, hand movements, or animation in order to make a clear solid connection. When you get the result you desired, follow up with praise.

Recommendations from
Susan Shoemaker, an autistic

Remember, you are looking for progress, *not* perfection.

CHAPTER 1

REMEMBERING THE EARLIEST YEARS IN MY LIFE

The Music Stopped

A white stuffed teddy bear plays the calming Brahms lullaby while the soft arm rays of sunlight shine through the wooden slats of the crib. The music fades; no sound remains. My little body trembles, tears flood my eyes, lips quiver, screaming, screaming, and screaming. Nobody comes; nobody, nobody comes.

The Spinning Metal Top

Pull up, push down, pull up, push down, pull up, push down. Around and around and around. Spinning faster, spinning faster, spinning faster. Pull up the red knob, push down the red knob, faster, faster, faster. Pull, push, pull, push, pull, push, spinning, spinning, spinning.

The Fisher Price Toy Radio

Turn the knob, turn the knob, turn the knob, "All around the vinegar jug, the monkey chased the weasel. The monkey thought t'was all in fun. Pop goes the weasel." Turn the knob, turn the knob, "All around the vinegar jug, the monkey chased the weasel." Turn the knob, turn the knob, turn the knob, "All around the vinegar jug, the monkey chased the weasel." Turn the knob, turn the knob, turn the knob, "All around the vinegar jug, the monkey chased the weasel." Turn the knob, turn the knob, turn the knob, "All around the vinegar jug, the monkey chased the weasel."

Mommy says, "Who's doing that? Susan, stop playing with that radio! You're going to break it!"

Turn the knob, turn the knob, turn the knob, "All around the vinegar . . ."

"Susan! Are you deaf?" she says. "Stop it! Give me that!"

Screams come. Kicking, banging, biting.

"Why did you take it from me, Mommy?"

The Jack-in-the-Box

Turn the handle, "Blink." Turn the handle, "Ba-blink." Turn the handle, "Ba-blink," turn the handle, "Ba-blinkity," faster, faster, faster. Turn the handle, "Blink-ba-blink-ba-blinkity-blink-ba-blink-ba-blink-ba-blink-ink. Ba-blink, ba-blink, ba-blinkity-blink. Blink! Blink-ba-blink-ink."

The clown puppet with the white head, white hands, and a blue cloth body pops up, pushing through the colorful lid of the metal box with the handle.

A Lady in the Music Box

Turn the key, turn the key, turn the key. The little lady with the little white dress and white slippers turns around and around and around to the sound of a tune. Close the box, the sound stops. Open the box, the sounds starts, and the little lady turns around and around and around. Close the box, open the box, close the box, open the box, close the box, open the box, close the box, open the box. Turn the key, turn the key, turn the key.

The Game of Trouble

Push the bubble, push the bubble, push the bubble. The game of Trouble has a bubble. Push the bubble, push the bubble, push the bubble. Hands flap. Hands clap. Push the bubble, push the bubble. Hands flap. Hands clap. Push the bubble. Hands clap. Push the bubble. Hands flap—

Mommy slaps. "Susan, stop that!"

Life's Spinning Wheel

Spin the spinner, spin the spinner, spin the spinner. Colors spinning, colors spinning, colors spinning. The Game of Life. Life has a spinner. Spin the spinner, spin the spinner—
"Susan, STOP IT!" Slap! "Take your turn; we want to play the game!"

Light Switch Flick

Click on, click off, click on, click off, click on, click off.
"Susan, stop playing with that light switch."
Click on, click off, click on, click off.
Smack. "Damn it! I said, leave it alone."

The Game of Jeopardy

Click, click, click, click, click, click, Mom's Jeopardy game has a clicker. "And the answer is . . ." Click, click. "And the answer is . . ." Click, click.
"Susan, stop making that noise. Give me that."

Rocking

Back and forth, back and forth, back and forth. There is no horse of course. Back and forth, back and forth, back and forth. A lost stare and no chair. Back and forth, back and forth, back and forth.
Mommy says, "What is wrong with you?"
Back and forth, back and forth, back and forth. Strange thing, there is no swing. Back and forth, back and forth, back and forth.
Mommy pushes on me. "Put those shoulders down and stop rocking. People are going to think you're odd."
To Mommy's dismay, my rocking stays. She tries every day to make it stop and go away.

Blocks with Faces

Matching faces, matching faces, matching faces. Flat white squares with a thick black circle, two eyes, a nose, and a mouth.

Mommy says, "Find the smile-face match. Find the angry-face match. Find the crying-face match. Susan, find the sneaky face—well, what are you waiting for? Susan, pay attention, not out in space somewhere. Come on, find the sneaky face. Susan, don't start that rocking again! Stop it. Just find the match!"

Screams come. Hand hits self along the head.

Mommy yells, "Stop it!"

Tears, kicking, throwing blocks. Mommy doesn't help me understand.

Sorting Colors

Box of eight, lay them straight; box of eight, lay them straight; box of eight, lay them straight. Big crayons, yellow, blue, red, green, orange, purple, black, and white. Big crayons, big crayons. Little crayons, little crayons, little crayons.

"What is this color?" "Aqua." "What is this color?" "Blue green." "What is this color?" "Maroon." "What is this color?" "Violet." "What is this color?" "Burnt sienna."

Tears come, feet stomp, hands shake, crayons fly. Sorting colors, big crayons, box of eight, lay them straight. Yellow, blue, red, green, orange, purple, black, and white.

Stay in the Lines

Stay in the lines. Stay in the line, stay in the lines. Watching Mother color with little crayons; she says, "Stay in the lines." Color, color, color; her picture looks right. Mine looks wrong. Big crayons, little crayons, little crayons, big crayons, little crayons. Coloring sessions remain until little crayons are now comfortable to use.

Tying Shoes

"Susan, come here. Dad wants to show you how to tie your shoes."

"You take the strings, like this, then make an X. No, no, one string in each hand and lay it down to make an X. No, no, like this. OK, take your fingers under this lace while taking your other fingers on this lace and pull.

"Let's start over. OK. That's better. Now you take the string and make a loop. Go around the tree. Come up through the hole. You try. No! No! Make a loop."

"Susan, you're not listening to your dad. Make a loop like this. OK. Now go around the tree."

Tears come.

Dad says, "What are you crying about? Go around the tree. Susan, stop crying!"

Tears fall, hands flap, feet kick—

"Susan, stop crying before I give you something to cry about! Put your feet back down on the floor! Stop waving your hands! Susan, settle down! Stop the damn screaming! What is wrong with you? Quit it! Stop biting!

"Helen, turn the cold water on in the bathtub! I'm tired of all these temper tantrums! I'm going to cool this hot head of hers down! Damn it, Susan!"

Days later, Mommy's turn. "Susan, get over here and sit down in front of me. Turn around."

Mommy's arms come around from behind me. She takes my right hand in her right hand, my left hand in her left hand. She says, "Hold this lace with these fingers." She taps her right hand on top of my right hand. She says, "Hold this lace with these fingers. She taps her left finger on my left hand.

She takes hold of my hands holding a lace in each. She says, "Cross over." Still holding, she crosses my hands. She pushes down on top of my shoe. "Let go of the lace." She shakes my hand. "Let go."

Still holding, she moves my left hand to my left side then releases this hand. She holds the top lace down with her left hand on the left side of the top lace. Her right hand still holding my right hand, she lifts up slowly, pulling towards us from under the top lace. She moves my right hand to my right side then releases it.

Mommy holds the end of the top lace. She says, "Susan, pay attention. Put your arm down and stop it. Susan, quit trying to hit yourself. You're going to learn how to tie these shoes!" She takes my hands again and crosses them over in front of me.

Screams come, biting, and tears.

"Stop it!" she yells. "Why are you so stubborn?"

Head whips and kicking. She picks me up, moves me to the middle of the floor. Then I slide out of her arms onto the floor.

Sometime much later, my Uncle Roger tries. Outside on the walk, he says, "Susan, come here. Sit down." He moves my feet; my toes touch his toes. He lifts my chin. "Susan, look at me. I want your hands to do the same thing my hands do."

Now, like a reflection in a mirror, moving in slow motion, he takes one lace. I take one lace. He takes the other lace; I take the other lace. He crosses the laces; I cross the laces. He tucked one under the other; I tucked one under the other. He pulled the lace out from under the other; I pulled one out from under the other. He pulled both ends at the same time; I pulled both ends at the same time. He made a loop; I made a loop. He pushed the lace up from under the lace around the loop; I pushed the lace up from under the lace around the loop. He pulled both loops at the same time to the right and to the left; I pulled both loops at the same time to the left and to the right. Shoes tied in five minutes.

Daddy says to Roger, "She ties her shoes backwards and upside down, Rog."

Roger says, "At least, they're tied."

Wrapped

My blanket is soft, warm, cuddly, and secure. I tear the binding off the edges. I pat my lips and tongue with the corner. I close my eyes. I wrap myself all over with it.

Mom says I look like a mummy. She pulls my blanket off my head. She says I am going to suffocate—a word with no meaning.

I grab it back.

Dad says by doing this, it cuts off oxygen to my brain.

My husband says, "You're a grown woman, not a little kid." He says, "Why do you flip your fingers with it?"

I say, "It's my *blankie!*"

He says, "It's a rag!"

I love my blankies and have had them for over thirty years. The old one is in pieces, but I use these for patting and flapping. My newer blankie is for wrapping.

Music in the Suitcase

Dad brings home a small suitcase. Inside a black circle, a knob, a lever, and a rectangle on a spring. There are holes to the side of this black circle. I touch the circle. It spins.

Dad says, "Susan, do not touch. I'm going to show you kids how to use a record player."

He takes the cord, plugs it in the wall. He puts a square box on the table. Inside, numbers on paper. Between the paper, he pulls out a flat, round orange thing.

He says, "This is called a record." He puts it on top of the black circle. He turns the knob; it clicks. He pulls the lever; the orange circle on the black circle spins. My hands flap. My hands clap.

I reach over to touch. I get slapped.

"Susan, I told you not to touch."

He puts the rectangle on the spring on the edge of the orange circle. The sound of music plays. "Andy on the move. Andy wont' rest. Andy Burnett, he's a-travelin' west." Spinning, spinning, spinning around and around and around. Musical sound, musical sound, musical sound. Hands flap; hands clap.

"Andy's on the move. Andy won't rest. Andy Burnett, he's a-travelin' west."

Hands flap; hands clap; spinning, spinning, spinning. All around, musical sound. Hands flap; hands clap.

Finding the Boundaries of Felt

In second grade, at Our Lady of Lourdes School, Mrs. Sullivan had a felt board and felt pictures: a house, a tree, a sun, a cloud, a girl, a boy, a dog, and many others.

Mrs. Sullivan said I could play with these soft pictures. I would every day at lunch. I would slide each piece through my fingers. I liked the softness of each one. The sun was my most favorite. I rubbed my fingers on this picture over and over and over.

On Friday, I put several pictures in my pocket. On Saturday, mom sees me playing with them.

With a loud voice, she says, "Susan, where did you get those?"

I start to cry.

She repeats, "Susan, I asked you, where did you get those?"

I struggle to get the words out but could not. She grabs all the pictures. I scream; I grab. I hit my head with my hand. She is taking the soft pictures away.

Soon, Dad comes into my room. He grabs my left wrist and drags me out into the hall. He picks me up then carries me to the kitchen. He sits me down. In a loud voice, he says, "Susan, your mother wants to know where you got these from." He points to the pile of felt pictures set on the table. He says, "Well, I'm waiting for an answer."

Tears are heavy in my eyes. My body is shaking, but the words would not come out.

Dad takes hold of both my shoulders as he looks at me. "Susan, look at me! Where did you get them?"

The only word that comes out is "school." He says, "Did you steal them? Susan, did you steal them?" Dad's voice is much louder now. "Did someone tell you you could have them?"

"Yes," I scream.

He goes on, "Who? Who, Susan?"

I look over at those soft pictures. Tears, tears, more tears.

Dad says, "Damn it! I want to know now!"

The only word that comes out is "teacher." He lets go of my shoulders and says, "You're lying; why would the teacher give them to you? Did she say you could bring them home? Well, did she?"

I begin rocking and waving my arms. Dad takes hold again. "Stop it right now! Did she say you could take these home?"

I say, "No—"

Dad stands straight up and says, "See? You're lying to me. Susan, your thinking is all backward. Get over here." He points at the floor in front of the mirror. He says, "We are going to get you going in the right direction, now!" He says, "Stand and face this mirror. I want you to look at yourself and say 'I am a liar.' Go on! Say 'I am a liar.'"

I am standing there so lost. Dad yells, "Look at yourself. Start saying 'I am a liar, I am a liar, I am a liar.'" Little by little, those words come out. I stand with my shoulders up, tears of sadness, and repeating words with no meaning: "I am a liar. I am a liar. I am a liar." Dad yells from the kitchen, "Susan, I can't hear you!" I scream, "I am a liar, I am a liar, I am a liar."

On Monday, my older brother walks me to my classroom with the felt pictures in a brown lunch bag. He tells the teacher as he hands her this bag, "My sister took these."

Mrs. Sullivan says it is stealing, and I will go to hell.

Clocks

Tick, tick, tick, tick, tick, tick. Wind the wristwatch back and forth, back and forth, back and forth. Grandpa's Big Ben, turn the key, turn the key, turn the key, ticktock, ticktock, ticktock. Grandma's cuckoo clock, ticktock, ticktock, ticktock. Mommy's wall clock, tick, tick, tick, tick, tick, tick. Daddy's new backward wall clock, "The Bar is Open"; turn the sign over, "The Bar is closed." The sound is right: tick, tick, tick. The numbers, "A Fright."

Telling Time

The *Today Show* is on at 7:00 AM. *Hollywood Squares* is on at 11:30 AM. Soap operas start at 1:00 PM., end at 3:00 PM. Local news at 6:00 PM, national news at 6:30 PM.

Dinner at 5:00 PM, bedtime at 9:00 PM, breakfast at 6:00 AM.

Hee Haw, Saturday at 7:00 PM. *Abbott and Costello,* Sunday at 11:30 AM. Cartoons, Saturday morning from 9:00 AM—12:00 PM. *Wild Kingdom,* Saturday Night. The Wonderful World of Walt Disney, Saturday night. Popcorn, soda pop, and pretzels. *Mash* at 7:00 PM.

Library opens at 9:00 AM. Banks open at 9:00 AM. Church at 11:00 AM. Lunch at 12:00 PM.

School, Monday to Friday. *Wide World of Sports,* Saturday. *Columbo* at 8:00 PM. Oprah at 4:00 PM. *The Match Game* at 3:00 PM. *Tattle Tales* at 3:30 PM. *Law & Order* at 7:00 PM. *American Justice* at 4:00 PM. *The Brady Bunch* at 7:00 PM. *Happy Days* at 8:00 PM. *Laverne and Shirley* at 8:30 PM. *Sesame Street* at 3:00 PM and 8:00 AM. *Gumby* at 7:00 PM. *Davy and Goliath* at 7:00 AM. *Popeye* at 6:00 AM. *The Little Rascals* at 3:00 PM. *Wonderama* at 11:00 AM on Sunday. *Starsky and Hutch,* 8:00 PM. *Baretta,* 8:00 PM. *The Rockford Files,* 8:00 PM. *McMillan & Wife,* 8:00 PM. *McCloud,* 8:00 PM. *Beat the Clock* at 7:00 PM. *Truth or Consequences* at 7:30 PM. *Wheel of Fortune* at 7:00 PM. *Jeopardy* at 7:30 PM. *The Dukes of Hazzard* at 8:00 PM.

Television shows were viewed by age or popularity. For example, a full-time mother, Mom watched television from six in the morning to eleven in the evening. With five bothers and Dad in the house, sports were very popular. My sister did not watch much television at home with the family, but rather, with her friends at their homes.

Daddy watched some sport events football, baseball, and especially *Bowling for Dollars* because he was a weekly bowler during the winter months. Also he liked *Hee Haw* as he was a country gent from Punxsutawney, Pennsylvania. Dad was a deer hunter, so hunting shows were a high interest for him. *Wild Kingdom, National Geographic,* and fishing shows made their way to the television line-up of shows. Brothers Bill, Tom, Mike, and Pete favored *Bugs*

Bunny, Tom and Jerry, The Monkeys, Scooby-Doo, Bugs Bunny, and *Wide World of Sports,* of course.

A variety of shows bouncing from what Mom watched to what Dad liked to what they enjoyed. Trust me, in a five-room house containing two bedrooms, a kitchen, a bathroom, and a living room (with a couch that turned into a bed for Mom and Dad), our house had five televisions: three small and one large (for video games) in the living room, and one in the kitchen for Mom. It was a big adjustment for someone with sensitive hearing. Sounds came from every direction, stimulating my senses and scrambling my head. Dad's insistence for me to socialize puts me in the small living room with this noise. I would rather be in my room.

Lost Celebrations

Holidays or special celebrations have always been very hard for me to understand. I know they are very important to others. I am not sure I know why.

For example, I remember my first communion. The girls wore white dresses, white shoes, white gloves, and white veils. The boys wore black pants, black shoes, black tie, black jacket, and white shirt. All the children walked down the middle of the rows to the priest (Father Davis). He said, "The body of Christ." We said, "Amen." Opened our mouth, stuck out our tongue. He placed a thin white round thing on my tongue. I walked over to the left of the row. After service, I was standing on the sidewalk outside the church watching people getting in cars. I was crying. Sister Mary Bernadette asked, "Susie, why are you crying?" The only word that came out was "Mommy." She called my mom, who soon came and took me home.

Another time, I went to a birthday party for a classmate, Annie. There were many boys and girls. Lots of red and white balloons, bubbles, and colorful wrapped presents. A rectangle cake with white icing outline with red swirls. The words "Happy 7th Birthday, Annie" in red letters with a face of Raggedy Ann was on the top. Seven pink candles were placed on the cake. Sounds of singing "Happy Birthday," sounds of cheer, laughter, words, and faces scared me. I ran to her swing set, sat on the slide, held my ears, rocked, and cried.

Ann's mother came over and asked, "Are you alright?" I looked to the side, at the tree. She said, "Please come and join us. Annie is going to open her presents now." She took my hand and walked me over to the table with presents. I cried some more and wet my pants. Later, my mom picked me up.

She said I embarrassed her by not caring about my friends, her, and wetting my pants.

Still another lost celebration was my eighth birthday, combined with my brother Tom's, as we are one year and five days apart. I did not like cake, but for Tom, Mom made a chocolate cake, chocolate icing.

That year, I got a KerPlunk game. The game consisted of a purple plastic tube with many small holes and several bigger holes. The tube was placed securely in a purple tray with four sections. The game had green, yellow, and pink long, thin sticks. You placed the sticks in one hole, and they came out in another. When all the sticks were put in place, clear marbles with colorful swirls were dropped through the top hole of this purple tube, dropping onto the colorful sticks. Each player slides one color stick out of the hole with the least number of marbles falling into their tray selection. The winner is the one with the least number of marbles after all the sticks had been removed.

The problem for me was too many color combinations: too confusing, too loud, and the marbles themselves reminded me of people's eyes—scary!

Mom said, "Susan doesn't appreciate anything we do for her." I think she said this because I went to my room after playing one game.

Christmas time was mixed. Sure, there was a tree with lights, decorations, and music: "Silent Night," "White Christmas," "Deck the Halls," "Frosty the Snowman," "Jingle Bells," and others. There was fruit cake (yuck!), cookies, candy, the meal, and Christmas characters.

However, on Christmas day, it was filled with sounds, expressions, and confusion. I spent part of this day putting order back in place. I would pick up wrappings, toys, clothes, or other gifts, placing each in rows according to size and age. For example, the bigger presents went toward the back of the Christmas tree; next, middle-sized presents; then on to the very smallest gift in front. The oldest started with Dad, then Mom, Bill, Deb, me, Tom, Mike, Pete, and the youngest, Steven:

Dad	Christmas tree trunk	Steven
Mom		Pete
Bill		Mike
Deb		Tom
	Me	

This arranging of items caused my mom to be angry. She would say, "Susan, would you stop organizing everything and play with your toys!"

Some presents had things to put in order. These, I liked best. There was the leather belt craft kit, the bead kit, the pot holder-making kit with colors to sort. I got dolls, but I did not really play with them. Instead, I patted their head, straightened their hair, moved their legs to sit, put their arms down, and turned their head to look up. This is the same way Mom took care of me. My sister would give her dolls voices. I did not. Christmas time was, at times, too confusing.

My graduation party from high school was a small pizza party at home with family. It did not make sense (and still does not). Why a cap, a gown, and a diploma are necessary? Why all the fuss?

Even baby showers, bridal showers, sweet sixteen birthday party, Super Bowl parties, Halloween parties, and many other events are hard for me to understand. Why this big need to celebrate? Why the need to make noise? Peace comes from inside oneself knowing you did the best you could.

School Days

Report card says, "Listening test, high average; problems with muscular control; disturbs group; does not listen with understanding; clumsy using crayons, scissors, easel, rhythm instruments. Does not understand what is being read. Susan is passively attentive in class and easily distracted. Does not have clear correct expression. Does not recognize words. Does not problem-solve. Cannot attack new words. Does not spell correctly. Susan's schoolwork improves with independent seating. Lacks self-confidence. Does not recognize numbers. Does not use self-control. Does not use her time well. Reading is becoming more  and more difficult for Susan. Susan does not use words when necessary."

Fourth-grade report card has nineteen unsatisfactory marks, Us; and eleven below average, Ds. The public school promoted me to the fifth grade anyway.

Fifth-grade report card shows I was given twenty-four average marks, Cs, due to a lengthy absence. Sixth-grade report card has nineteen unsatisfactory marks, Us; and seventeen below average marks, Ds. Again, I was promoted to the next grade level, seventh.

Throughout my remaining school years, I took the locals classes as regents was too hard. Photography, woodshop, ceramics, interior design, home economics, art, drafting, basic television, advanced television, earth science, movies, and many other hands-on courses offered at the various schools attended. I did receive a high school diploma but only had a third-grade reading level and a third-grade math level.

Radio Reruns

My dad was concerned about my imagination not developing like the other children. He said I was too serious and lacked any imaginary play.

One Friday evening, Mom and Dad returned home from shopping. Daddy said, "Susan, go get your tape recorder." He came into my bedroom, which I share with my sister. He had a cassette called "Edgar Bergen and Charley McCarthy." My brothers came in to join us.

"What do ya got?" Tom said.

Dad said, "I want you kids to listen to this. Before television was invented, all that people had was their radio to listen to. Your mother and I saw this, and we thought you would get a kick out of it."

Lost, I sat on the bed rocking. Daddy put the cassette player on the dresser. My sister sat next to me. I don't want her sitting next to me. I push her away.

She tells Dad, "Susan's pushing me again." Dad turns around and tells me to stop it.

My shoulders lift up and tears come. Dad says, "Stop your damn crying and listen." He put the cassette in the player. A man begins talking about old-time radio shows and the problems they had.

Then the music begins. The show is filled with conversations, jokes, and singing. I turn my head sideways and listen. I am fixated.

This was the start of many more shows that followed. I listened to that cassette 169 times. Dad brought a second cassette home: "Inner Sanctum Mysteries—Only the Dead Die Twice." Again and again and again, I listened to these two cassettes.

Later, Mom saw an ad in her TV Guide magazine to purchase more shows. My brother Mike would let me deliver his daily newspaper when it was too hot, raining and cold, or he was lazy. He would pay me fifty cents a day. I saved my money until I earned $34. Mom wrote a check for me. Soon, I owned nine more shows.

Once, while on the book mobile flipping through records, I saw *The War of the Worlds* old radio show. After that, I went to the library regularly to get records or cassettes with radio shows. I even got some books with facts about who played who, the names of characters, the broadcasting network, and the year. I copied much information in a journal I still have today.

Over the years, I have collected over four hundred shows. I continue to enjoy them even today. My husband does not understand the bond. However, my son does. He, too, enjoys listening. *The Baby Snooks Show* is his favorite.

Word Play

My sister would call me a pain. I would get mad, thinking, what is a pain? Why are you calling me that? I would push my upper and lower teeth together, reach out and pinch her. She would call to Mom and I would be slapped on the hand for doing this.

In second grade, the teacher taught me about window panes. When my sister continued to call me a pain, I thought she was calling me a window. I would become much more angry with her—hitting her or kicking at her—because she made no sense. I had always been told I was the one who did not make sense. Why would someone call another person a window?

It was not until many years later (in grown-up times), I realized that there was more than one meaning to a word—also more than one way to spell a word.

Another example of this: Daddy and Mom took all us kids on vacation. At one part of our stay in the trailer, sirens of emergency vehicles came close to the campgrounds. There were lots of excited people running in all directions.

Soon, Dad came inside to tell Mom what all the fuss was about. He said, "There was a man who was trying to shoot—son."

I thought how odd it would be if all people had to live in darkness—if we no longer had the sun. For years, I was bothered by this idea of living with no natural light. It wasn't until my early forties that I realized my fears were not real; that in fact, if I had at the time known the difference between these completely different words with different meanings, my stress would have been greatly reduced.

Also, if I were not crippled by background noise, I might have heard the missing word to the statement "There was a man who was trying to shoot their son." In short, I decided it is very important to make a list of words that sound the same yet are spelled differently and mean different things:

see—sea
aunt—ant

son—sun
pane—pain
blue—blew
flew—flu
flower—flour
dear—deer
wine—whine
red—read
won—one
wood—would
soul—sole
tail—tale
mare—mayor
pale—pail
meet—meat
knight—night
hear—here
fair—fare
knew—new
might—mite
made—maid
write—right
main—mane
two—too—to
die—dye
hare—hair

To add to the already complicated use of words that can cripple, there are words that are spelled the same and mean different things:

lead (visual)—a thin stick of marking substance in or for a pencil lead
(action)—to guide on a way especially by going in advance

bark (visual)—the tough exterior covering of a woody root or stem
bark (action)—the sound made by a barking dog

lie (visual)—the haunt of an animal
lie (action)—to assume a horizontal position

Words continuously are a constant problem in understanding another person's intentions. Simplifying life is how I survive with the least amount of stress or confusion.

The next few pages may help others to understand how I work. Keep in mind: rules, order (list), routine, or simple commands give me a direction in which to process new information slowly in my world of *absolutes*!

OPPOSITES

backward		forward
up		down
left		right
fast		slow
day	dawn, dusk	night
hot		cold
solid		liquid
black		white
positive		negative
sweet		sour
top	middle	bottom
male		female
young		old
live		die
short		long
wet	damp	dry
heaven		hell
high		low
quiet		noisy
soft		hard
near		far
fantasy		reality
awake		asleep
walk		run
sit		stand
north		south
east		west
agree		disagree
stop		go
AM		PM

good		evil
strong		weak
new		old
peace		war
dirty		clean
organized		disorganized
early		late
cheap		expensive
heavy		light
push		pull
in		out
empty		full
pretty		ugly
win		lose
in		out
hi		bye
open		close
right		wrong
begin		end
start		finish
tiny		huge
small	medium	large
thin		fat
rich		poor
on		off
alive		dead
truth		lie
fact		fiction
smart		dumb
light		dark
reward		punishment
internal		external
enter		exit
past	present	future
conscious		unconscious

The world works through opposites: for every action, there is an equal and opposite reaction. However, a transition (or a third component) is necessary to complete the process.

Look at these examples.

The Seasons in the Year

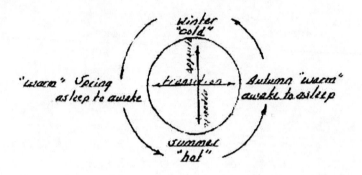

cold → warm → hot → warm → cold
     3 parts   3 parts

Math works the same. Two addends equal a sum:

$$0 + 1 = 1$$
$$1 + 1 = 2$$
$$1 + 2 = 3$$
$$1 + 3 = 4$$
$$1 + 4 = 5$$

All of these have three parts.

A yardstick has three parts:

1 ft	2 ft	3 ft

A Clock

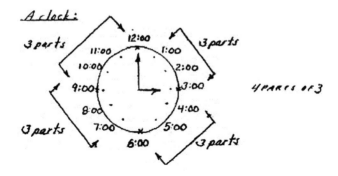

Time moves from right to left; the seasons, from left to right.

A Traffic Light

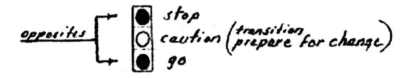

An Egg

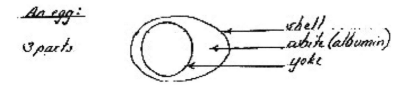

Reproduction

Two entities, male and female
Egg + sperm = fertilization, to produce offspring

Pregnancy

Three trimesters

Human beings have three parts:

Mind, body, and soul
Skeletal, muscular, nervous system

Solid—Liquid—Vapor

Colors

Black (all colors present), white (all colors absent)

Three primary colors: red, blue, and yellow

Red + blue = purple
Blue + yellow = green
Yellow + red = orange

Religion

Father, Son, Holy Ghost
Three wise men

*When Christ died on the cross, he was in the middle, and one on each side—a total of three.

Music

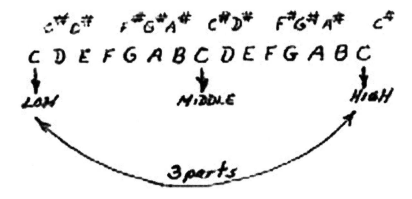

The minor scale is made up of three forms: normal (or pure minor), the melodic minor, and the harmonic minor.

The illustration shows how musical notes can be broken down into a simple form containing three parts. Music has built off of this into more complex processes.

Telephone Keypad

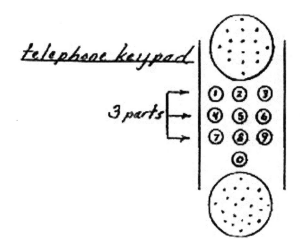

CHAPTER 2

"FOR THE LOVE OF SUSIE"

Chapter 2 introduces us to the "love of Susie." It provides the reader with an understanding of who Susie is, her learning style, and how confused she becomes when trying to understand the different meanings of words.

Throughout this chapter, Susie refers to facial expressions, body language, and tone in trying to make sense of this crazy world in which we live.

Not only does Susie introduce us to who she is, but she also introduces us to her parenting abilities, self-confidence, and abuse she may have suffered as a child. The only problem is that Susie only knows of it as being abuse when she is told that that is what it was. She is still confused as in her mind, she doesn't see it as child abuse.

Susie lives in a world of constant confusion and disruption. She has been described as having unusual behaviors and very poor communication skills. Part of this behavior is based on the fact that Susie is not able to let go of past things or an incident that may have occurred. Whether it was today, yesterday, or ten years ago, it is still fresh in her mind, and she is still trying to make sense of it. Pictures of the past and scrambled conversations play over and over in Susie's mind as she continually tries to make sense of this crazy world she lives in

CHAPTER 2

Just thought I would tell you because no one seems to be interested in getting to know me except me. No one seems to have time to listen to the stories of my experiences, which have great lessons of truths about people and the selfish things people say and do.

I'm not looking for pity (that only makes things worse). I'm looking for answers to finding myself, my place in this interesting world of assorted pictures and words. I know I'm important too, but talking to others only seems to cause me so much conflict, and the things that people do—are sometimes fun and interesting but mostly a mystery that leads to questions that I have no immediate answers to or understanding of.

I know about most rules, which makes my life easier. I do not see the world the same as most people do. This is okay because I have my own world inside of me that is safe and full of beautiful gifts of love—a quality that few people seem to have. My world is simple and pure, not full of the harsh, mean, and demanding rituals of society. I express myself in small, little baby steps, which many folks do not see unless they are close to me. Again, as I just said, people do not seem to have time for me or even the interest in getting to know the love of Susie.

Before I begin, keep in mind as I talk about myself that the stories will be discussed in the order of which the picture memories connect with the words as I write, so there is not a particular order of a beginning or an end, but rather, a continuous series of events in which my experiences occur each and every day in my mind. Remember, too, that my emotions are delayed during most of the actual journeys; however, some are simply reactions to the facial expressions, tones, or words of others; and finally, some of my emotions are true to the picture, whether it is sad, happy, or mad. I will let you know as we go.

Yesterday, Gary (that's my handsome husband) and I were discussing about me coming from another planet, and that aliens dropped me off on earth because nobody there could talk to me because I made no sense. I told Gary that I simply never could understand what all the fuss was about when women get excited about men's butts, and men get excited about women's hooters.

He said that I was inappropriate to make that statement to my former English teacher and friend, Mr. Odum. He said I was inappropriate to make this statement to Mr. Ike (the driver on the school bus I matron on), and it was wrong to say it to the nice David and Garth (two more bus drivers), and to Rob Horey (the temporary family therapist). In short he said not to ask a man that question, or to make a comment about it again to a man. He said that these people are taking their index finger and flipping their lips up and down in disbelief, wondering what planet I came from.

Gary did ask me what I look for in a person, especially a man. I said that I look really quick at their eyes and facial expression, then their hair, their clothes (really the colors they are wearing), and finally, I listen to their voice. (Is it soft or loud? Do they speak connecting words together? Do they smile while they are speaking?)

Gary's response was anything but reassuring. He laughed louder and longer, but stated this was why he loved me. I must say I still did not get an answer to my question, and several more filled my thoughts. I do know that I won't bring up that question to a man again because even though this is a rule of which I have no understanding, it is safer than being told I'm from another planet. And I suppose that the safest thing for me to do if someone else brings it up is to say nothing and just think of it as words with no meaning. This makes no sense to me, but what can I do?

Earlier in the day, I had experienced the same sort of unanswered questions with Mike, my handsome fourteen-year-old son. It started with a simple knock on his door to let him know it was nine in the morning, time to get up. His response was anything but pleasant. His tone and words of "I know!" made me question myself as to whether or not I had done something wrong and still another question of "How do I fix it?"

I took a few moments to rethink about how my tone and actions were toward him. Was I not nice enough, or was I to be more firm in requesting that he get up?

I decided to try again by sweetly and concernedly reminding him that it was time to take his medicine. I suppose my reluctance to be more firm was due to my not wanting to get nervous that early in the morning, especially since I woke up feeling so rested and calm.

I again went to his door and sweetly said, "Sweetie, I just remembered you have to take your medicine."

Mike now insisted that he was not happy by firmly stating, "I know, Mother!"

Now for me, this tone and the words triggered an immediate command of words. "Mike, get up and start your day. It's getting late!" I was now aware of my nerves. They seemed to be pulsing inside of me, and I walked into the living room and sat down, picked up my coffee cup, and began to arrange in order the chores of the day.

Mike came out of his room with an expression of unhappiness followed by a steady stream of questions and statements, which I tried to respond to in the order that he said them. First was "There is no cereal in the house, so I guess I can't eat breakfast!"

I suggested in a calm response, "There is bread for toast, and I think there are a few eggs."

Mike now firmly stated, "I don't feel like cooking!"

For me, this felt like a failure in my role as a nurturing mother, but I sat quietly drinking my coffee and redirecting my focus back to the day's agenda when another verbal message was ordered at me: "I am going to take a shower this morning!"

I immediately stopped my focus and entered into Mike's because part of my Friday's routine was doing the laundry, and I certainly was not going to do laundry late into the afternoon, nor was I going to set myself up to get yelled at when the water pressure dropped while he was in the shower. So I told Mike very directly (knowing full well I was in for a nasty response), "I want you to take your shower now; I have laundry to do!"

Mike returned a remark, just as I had predicted: "Jesus Christ, I can't relax at all around here!"

Now I was shaking with fear but responded with a loud "Mike!"

Mike stomped into the bathroom and slammed the door. Again, I felt I did the wrong thing. How was I to fix this awful problem of communicating in a bad way?

I know it has to be hard for everyone in this house to live with such broken, disconnected, unhappy messages of words. I suppose if I weren't so sensitive to the responses of others or their words, life for them would be easier. However, if I weren't sensitive to their feelings, both Mike and Gary would think I didn't care; and that makes no sense to me. After all, I was raised by boys. And for boys, Susan was better at doing what she was told than she was at speaking or being herself.

This was a rule that was clearly arranged for me by my parents, and I am not sure if it makes sense all the time.

For now, anyway, looking for an answer to that question is the least of my worries. My son will be leaving on the eleventh of April for the Pathways therapeutic foster care program—a very scary change for me and for Mike. At this time, I shall not discuss any further thoughts on the subject because it just hurts too much; and besides, only time and a lot of prayer will hold the answers to our fears. Again, rules make life easier for me, and these rules of time and prayer definitely make sense.

Well, several events took place today. I talked to my brother Tommy. He is one year and five days younger than I am. He is very much like me in his way of thinking. We talked a great deal about cartoons and *The Little Rascals*, laughing about the one-liners that Foghorn Leghorn said and, of course, the other characters.

We talked about being parents and about our parents. This topic makes me so uncomfortable, and—well, I guess hearing about my childhood made me question my own abilities to be a good parent, especially since I'm not sure anymore about my own parents' style of raising children. I have so much understanding of why my parents treated me the way they did, especially my Mom.

Some people believe that I was abused, but I do not have a clear idea in my mind as to what to do with that knowledge even if it were true. I do know, however, that doing the same type of correcting methods for Mike is not a choice I wish to do; nor have I ever done them. My questions of parenting abilities lie more in the area of balance and responses and letting go (letting Mike learn even if he gets hurt). If I do make choices, they are often based on rules; and sometimes, when I make a decision, I often question myself as to whether or not it was the right thing.

As Tommy and I continued to talk, memories of events and conversations of my youth played over and over in my mind. It was like someone kept hitting the rewind button on a tape recorder or turning the reverse lever on a movie projector.

I'm not sure if I needed any questions answered. I had simply accepted every part of my childhood, especially since it was quite understood that I had the unusual behaviors and very poor communication skills.

However, Tommy insisted that the way I was treated by the whole family was wrong. He had even stated, "I disagree with you, Sue. Mom and Dad had no right to put you under the cold water in the bathtub. It was child abuse, plain and simple!"

Again, the words *child abuse*, and again were the questions "What do I do with this knowledge? Am I supposed to feel something? What can be done about it now? Should I do something about it?" The chain of questions simply continued through my thoughts, and I had now taken notice of the time on the clock. It was 1:24, and I remembered Tommy said he was leaving at 1:30 to take the family ice-skating.

We wound up the conversation with the promise that we would speak again at a later time.

I now sat on the couch and was replaying the words of the phone conversation with Tommy when a car door closing brought my focus to the front door, where I saw Mike and Miss Magee (Mike's tutor) coming up the walk. They had spent several hours at the library working on a research paper for his school studies. A short time later, she had left the house, and Mike and I were alone.

I questioned myself as to whether or not I should share my phone conversation with Mike. I decided to share it because I was so pleased just to have the opportunity to talk with Tommy.

As I began to share my experience (repeating word for word), Mike looked at me with a soft smile and his hand in the air (like a policeman stopping traffic). I knew it was a topic of which he did not want to hear anymore about.

Well, now I could only sit and wait for Gary to come home; maybe he would be interested in sharing my delightful phone visit with Tommy. Mike had informed me that he was tired and was going to lie down and take a nap.

I focused my attention on the TV while I waited for Gary. *The Rockford Files* caught my eye. This was a show my mom was very fond of. I decided to watch it. After all, Tommy and I were just talking about our childhood.

Shortly into the program, I heard Gary coming in the driveway. I was happy for many reasons. I met him outside, although his facial expression was not like mine. He was angry-looking; and his tone, along with his words, was completely dissatisfied with his day's work.

I knew I had not done anything wrong, and I knew I could not fix what had already happened; however, I could help him try to put a smile on his face by helping him take the board out of the van and later telling him of my conversation with Tommy.

Gary continued to grumble about different things as we worked together to get my punch car out of the garage. At one point, Gary's tone was so mean and nasty that I refused to continue to help by responding with a chain of repeated words from past conversations. Shortly after walking away, I returned to help with a smile on my face because I came to the understanding that he was doing this clumsy hassle of getting the car out for me since he knew I had waited a long time to drive it.

Once the car was out, I looked it over with a feeling of joy. My punch car, my 1973 Super Beetle Volkswagen. A car I had always wanted since I was a child on a school bus looking out the window at all the punch bugs one could find on our short trip to and from school. I got inside, and a twinkle came to my eyes. At that moment, an almost lifelong dream had come true. I was behind the wheel of a punch car, and I could hardly wait to drive it.

Gary was not there at that moment, but I know he could never fully understand my interest in old things, certainly not with an item of no great monetary value. Still it was my dream come true, and I could see so many visions of pictures flash through my thoughts. Some were with Mike learning to drive it and later taking it on his own to school. I could see him and I working together on the engine (since it is one of the simplest engines ever made), to washing and waxing of the exterior. I could see smiles on his friends' faces and, mostly, Mike's face shining with happiness as he will be one of the first juniors or seniors in high school with a car that has all the features of a true boy toy. However, if for some reason, Mike decides this car is too much for him, at least I can delight in having my dream a reality.

Now Gary entered the driveway again with the air compressor; and within no time at all, we had the tire blown up, the license plates bolted on, and were driving my beautiful punch car. Wow, what a feeling!

A little time later, we were home again, but I tried to hold on to the two wonderful pieces of happiness that had entered into my day: Tommy and the punch car, which were quickly scrambled away by conversations at the dinner table.

First, Mike did not feel well because his ear was bothering him. I told him I was going to call the doctor on Monday, and that was that. Mike did not seem pleased. However, Mom knows that this problem was brought to my attention almost a week ago, and now I had no choice but to have a doctor tell us if there is something to worry about.

The next part of the conversation had been about Tommy since I had waited almost four hours to share my joy with Gary. He was less than happy for me. He stated that my whole family was a bunch of closet cases.

When he says things like that, it makes me sad because I was not asking for answers. I was simply repeating my experience; the understanding of the words will come later. Certainly, the last thing I need is to have someone else's focus of words enter into my thoughts. I do not want to play follow the leader anymore. I want to smash the mirror and have a self that others will accept. Besides, like Gary always says, "Susie's different, but she's harmless!"

My thoughts were flooding with questions, statements, and pictures—ones that seem to make sense.

Then the phone rang. It was Nicole (a friend of Mike's). This was the first contact with any of his friends from school since he went into Brylin Hospital in

November, and now it was the end of March. I was so panicked inside because now another flood of old memories from these last six months raced through my head, as if someone has rewound the video tape back to a year ago and now was playing it on fast forward. Everything that had been heard, seen, and felt had come in just seconds of the voice on the other end of the phone. Now I was to make a decision to let Mike speak to her.

I turned my focus to Gary. I told him who was on the phone and calmly asked, "Can Mike talk to her?" He replied, "Yes." However, I told Mike he could only talk for ten minutes. He took the phone and began a conversation.

I, on the other hand, was now filling my thoughts with hundreds of questions: "What if he asks me why I didn't tell him she had called many times before?" "What if it was not really Nicole (since Mike had mixed me up before with different names to the voices)?" "What did I really know about Nicole?" I had met her a few times, and she seemed nice, but Mike said she was a liar and a slut. Was this true? Gary liked her, but then, Gary always liked pretty girls.

Was this to be another hide-and-seek game or a push-comes-to-shove game? What was this whole teenager thing about? Was Mike going to hate me more when I try to set rules? Was Mike going to break the rules, and if he did, what would I do? Was Gary finally going to help me raise Mike instead of letting Mike run around with his peers with no supervision or very little supervision?

Hundreds of questions filled my thoughts in those ten minutes, and now it was time to tell Mike to get off the phone. I told myself to just try to stay as short as possible in answering his questions, knowing he would immediately demand a response. I was very nervous but spoke firm and short: "Mike, one more minute!"

Mike got off the phone and instantly demanded to know, "Why didn't you tell me Nicole called before?"

I told him that with everything that had happened in this past year, and especially with all the changes since his visit to the hospital, Gary and I felt it was best to wait until we got more help for the situation before allowing his friends to come back into the picture.

Mike's remark was not happy. He said, "Alright, I don't need a goddamn dissertation."

I hate that word, probably because I don't know what it means. But I did snap back at him: "Mike!"

Mike continued to make negative comments under his breath, to which my response was now triggered to a high pitch of panicky words.

Gary sat in the dining room and said nothing. Mike went into his room upset with me and, perhaps, the whole situation.

Now inside of me, I was beating myself hard for hurting Mike's feelings. I wondered if I had done the wrong thing again, yet at that very moment realized that I certainly could not raise Mike alone when there are two adults in the home. My rules and responses were truly not meant to make Mike feel bad. They were my only way of protecting him from other people's unsafe actions and words.

I went to Mike's door and knocked and then let myself in. I had to try to explain again how much Mom loves him, by saying the following: "Gary lets you run around on your own because he doesn't want to be bothered with raising you. Your friends get to run around unsupervised because their parent or guardian does not want to be bothered. Mom sets rules because she loves you, and that comes straight from my heart."

With these statements made, I left his room, and my eyes looked at Gary. I guess I had felt sad because he had not been there all these years to help me with Mike, and the words I had just spoken to Mike began a chill of truth throughout my body. How could Gary not care about Mike? He had promised to protect us and take care of us so many years ago.

Now more and more questions kept popping into my thoughts. "Had Gary lied?" "Why would people say things that aren't true?" "What was wrong with me?"

I decided that I had to share what I've started writing down just two days ago up to page eleven. Maybe then, Gary could help me understand why so many times, when I talk to people, I just can't seem to say the right thing. It only makes people mad or sad.

Well, Gary read what I had written up to page eleven and then started to laugh, saying, "See, honey, that's it. You don't understand!"

I began to repeat statements and experiences we shared in an effort to find the answer to the questions: "Do you care about Mike?" "Did you lie to me then, or are you lying now?" and, finally, the biggest, most important "If you have always known that I didn't understand, then why did you make decisions for us that hurt Mike and me?"

My eyes filled with tears as he spoke the most terrible words in the world: "You're crazy!"

Words from my past repeated over and over in my head: "Susan's stupid!" "Susan doesn't know what you're talking about!" "Susan's a blockhead!" "Your sister Sue is crazy!" "Your sister is stupid!" "Is your wife a retard?"

Over and over, the words played in my head, but I was not going to let memories take away from my love for Mike. I love him, and now he was going away from me because of me not knowing how to communicate with people. I told Gary I need him so much to work with the Pathways program, and with me, and of course, with Mike; because to me, Mike has been my strength even in the worst of times.

It is now Easter Sunday evening, twenty-four hours since the awful battle—words to let my family know that I am facing conflicts of deep concern about Mike leaving and of Gary's lack of support when I need him the most.

CHAPTER 3

SUSIE'S WORLD OF ROUTINE

Chapter 3 describes how Susie tries to make sense out of the world in which she lives. Susie lives by routine, order, patterns, and directions. Susie only understands black and white; simple and pure. She becomes very confused when something is in the gray area. She doesn't know how to make sense out of complex things.

The reader will learn in this chapter that even though Susie prefers to live a simple life, she is also a very amazing woman as this chapter describes how Susie learned to drive a school bus. To some of us, this could be a very frightening and complicated process; but to Susie, it is a matter of learning by the softness of tone, by steps that lead to success, and by performing the same hands-on function day after day.

Becoming a bus driver has been one of the best decisions in Susie's life as it has enabled her to meet new friends, learn to develop different trust levels in relationships, learn more about sports and life in general; and the best part of her job is that she works with children, whom she loves very much.

CHAPTER 3

I just feel quite sad sometimes about the changes that took place in recent years, along with the changes we are about to face—too, too many. My understanding is so strong in many ways, yet so lacking in ways that matter the most.

Mike and Gary almost always seem to want to help me where and when I don't need them and never seem to think much about helping me in the areas where I do need them. I try hard to explain, and then they either laugh at or correct me. I think there is no one who will ever know who Susie is except me; and this is why I am writing about my thoughts and experiences, in the hope I will someday see a pattern or a picture that will make some sense to me rather than having others scrambling me with more and more words of conversation with little to no meaning, or even sending messages of words with no picture to connect with.

It is Monday morning, about five o'clock; I'm looking forward to going to work, as I always do. Gary's alarm clock just went off; so it's time to go in the bedroom, turn on the lights, make the bed, give Gary a kiss, go push open Mike's door, and very gently say, "Good morning." (The gentleness is because with Mike, he can tend to be very nasty with his tone of voice, and I certainly am not going to be snapped at for being anything but gentle.)

And now, it is time to play my harp. This seems to be the only thing that has ever come naturally to me, yet when words from others in the room speak above a whisper (even if it is good) or if others have facial expressions of anything but smiles, I simply cannot play. Of course I have only had the harp for a few weeks shy of a year, but still I knew that from the first day I played a song and never having played an instrument before or taken a lesson, this was a natural gift (even if I did play it correctly for the first two weeks then felt better playing it backwards).

I tried to play a couple of songs just now; however, Gary's comment from one week ago keeps replaying over in my memory. What he said was "God, honey, can't you play something new? You play the same songs over and over and over! Jeez!"

I guess it does not mean much to him that I can play ninety-one songs from memory, even if they are just children's and Christmas songs. Still I cannot play when he is close by for the time being because he is so very loaded with worries of the new house.

See, I've only ever had two problems with Gary: his greed and his mouth. The greed comes from being an only child, being his own boss, and yelling louder to get what he wants. The problem I have with his mouth is he talks too loud, too fast, and too much.

If one were to look at some patterns of why Gary is like this, then the answer is simple: Like many people who drive their vehicle alone, they often enjoy the company of the radio and, in many cases, turn the volume up loud. Over time (months and years), a person's hearing may become affected by this constant pattern of loud noise. This is just the case for Gary. Truly, his hearing ability is greatly reduced, so now he speaks louder than an average person does.

The problem with me is that my hearing is too good. Gary talks too fast, and this is because of his thirty-six years of being his own boss and moving from one customer to the next, trying to keep them happy. Sometimes, Gary must talk loud and fast to get money owed to him or, as he says, "to keep from being screwed!" Again, knowing the pattern makes the answer to the question simple; however, I did not come to an understanding of this until within this last year.

Everything that Gary said and did before this was taken just as another day even though inside my head, many questions with no answers were swimming around. Gary has lowered his voice so much since a tiny piece of plastic called a hearing aid came into his life almost two years ago. Gary has slowed down his talking very much since he understood that I just have quite a time trying to respond with the correct statements.

Anyway, we're all under a lot of stress, as I said before, due to all of the changes. The new house is looking better and better all the time, especially because it is in the country, where it will be nice and quiet.

It's now time to head to work; and I enjoy my trips to and from because I am alone with my Charley Pride cassette, music my Dad listened to every Sunday morning before we went to church when I was a child. Work is fun too. In fact, the greatest thing I ever learned to do in my thirty-nine years of age was to learn how to drive a school bus.

My primary teacher was Ella. She is so wonderful. She smiled softly, and her voice was calm as she talked me through each step of learning to drive the bus. She did not mix up the order of which one needs to learn: from turning the key to proper placement of your feet while shifting gears to parallel parking to backing up.

She did not get upset with me at all; and yet after I took my road test, passed it, and got my CDL, she told me that if I was not able to understand what I needed to learn in the first two weeks of training, she would have had to let me go. Her concern then was, as she said, "I wonder if you have any common sense."

Anyway, she and many other trainers at the bus garage are the reason I did the greatest thing in my life: driving a school bus. I suppose the reasons for this joy are simple: First, there are many rules, especially about safety. It is also a hands-on job; and it's the same thing every day, just like when I was a child riding every day out into the world, even though I hated the school that I attended. The only problem I have with this job is, although I love children and I love driving the bus, I find it hard many times to put the two together.

Shortly after I joined the crew of drivers, we had a handicap training class, for which I signed up. So it was there I talked to my boss, Alta (another nice person), about my learning disability and said how much I would like to work on the handicap bus even if I was a matron. Well, to my delight, Alta decided over the weekend about the conservation on Saturday, and she allowed me to become a matron the following Monday. Wow, it was as if blessings were coming left and right! Now I was a matron working (or rather, it seems more like playing) with the children on the way to and from their schools.

Since my one and a half years of working, many more blessings have come my way. I have met so many people of different backgrounds and am learning so many wonderful things every day—about raising children, about friendship, about trust, about sports (mostly golf), about buses, about routines, about husbands, about wives, about the weather, about television, and an endless variety of subjects. The speed in which I am learning is truly fast. Sometimes, so fast I can't seem to keep up with much of the understanding or meaning of what is being said. This is okay because, as long as people continue to smile, it keeps me happy inside.

Now the children on my special need bus also are teaching me wonderful things like playing, sharing, caring, trust, friendship, and so many other acceptable skills.

CHAPTER 4

"THE MAN IN THE MIRROR"

Chapter 4 describes Susie's favorite time of the day: early morning, when she gets up for work, and everyone else around her are still in bed. Susie loves quiet time as it offers her peacefulness and calmness—a chance to escape to a simpler time. Susie is not one who can handle stress and chaos and the hustle and bustle of the world. She prefers no talking, no rushing, no screaming, no blaring of music, and no sounds. During her early morning routine, she is able to relax and get lost in the peacefulness of the quietness of the house. This is a time when she can reflect on the present, past, future.

Also in this chapter, Susie introduces us to "the man in the mirror," a colleague of hers, Mr. Ike (bus driver). Susie becomes very close to this man, but she does not allow him in to invade her private territory or become too close to him on a personal level. Susie keeps her distance from Mr. Ike and only converses with him through the mirror as this is a safe place for her. If she breaks away from the safety of the mirror and tries to converse with him on a more personal level, face-to-face with eye contact, this would be very difficult for her as Susie is not very confident when it comes to controlling her emotions or using her communication skills.

CHAPTER 4

It's now Tuesday morning at 5:00 AM. I have already turned on the light in the bedroom, made our bed, kissed Gary, opened Mike's door, and gently said, "Good morning." I am always pleased about this part of my day even though I get up somewhere between 3:30 and 4:00 AM. I enjoy the time spent alone.

You know how it is: no talking, no one rushing you in the shower, nobody in the upstairs apartment screaming at the child or blasting their music. No television, no telephone, no dog barking next door, no sounds of annoying volumes at all entering my sensitive hearing.

I do not have anything to rush through, only simple (in the dim lighting) relaxation. I can completely direct my thoughts to my focus and no one else's. I can put together the events of the day. I can reflect to a time in my past. I can dream about the future. I can think about good things or bad (if I choose). I can sing to myself within my thoughts. I can stare into that wonderful pocket of air and not have to worry if someone is going to slap me, laugh, or interrupt. I can think about people or places or things.

Yes, this is my time, and it is worth getting up at three thirty in the morning, Monday through Friday. It definitely sets a routine and allows me to relax completely within myself before the day moves into a fast-speed overload of my senses.

So now I'm at work again, sitting on my bus, waiting for Mr. Ike (my driver). It is so much fun here at work. Most folks are always smiling, especially my favorite people, Garth, David, Connie, Ella, and Danny (he is a mechanic who also helped train me to drive a bus). All the rest of these folks are bus drivers just like me.

I think at this time, I would like to talk about Mr. Ike.

Now let me say that the reason I call him Mister is this: Early in my days of working with him, all the children on our bus called him Mr. Ike, so in time, it seemed to be the most logical name for him. The children respected him, and now so did I (even though his first name is RC).

Although he and I talk quite a bit about many different subjects, including spouses, children, and past and present events, I can only talk to him by looking at him in the mirror. He sometimes looks in the rearview mirror, and this is when I ask him questions and make statements. For me, this is a safe and secure space for us to visit each other in conversation.

I find Mr. Ike to be a friendly and fun fellow who loves to have a good time (as long as no one gets hurt). He is a family man and comes from a large family (fifth youngest out of thirteen children). He is a spiritual man and a kindred spirit. I enjoy watching him play with the children on the bus. He is just super (a natural entertainer). He is a man who has a great deal of wisdom due to his past experiences (after all, he is 65 years old). He is a quiet, peaceful individual who is easy to talk to.

However, he is still only a man in the mirror (a reflection), a person I could never look at face-to-face except for very rare exceptions, and only for a few brief moments. The reason may be because I'm not sure of my emotions, or maybe I'm not sure of his; but emotions are something I have never been completely in touch with, only of fact-based words and order.

Not long ago, I had a picture image of me giving Mr. Ike a hug. I had a strong need to connect with this, so I asked him, "May I give you a hug?"

He agreed, and for a few short seconds, I squeezed him and then returned to my seat. I'm not sure what I felt, but I looked in the mirror for a moment and saw him wiping a few tears from his eyes. I suddenly felt as if I did the wrong thing because I made him cry.

The next day, however, something so very odd happened (odd in that it was as if Mr. Ike's sense of spirit and humor had now become a part of me). I told him about my handsome husband's clumsy action of stepping in dog poop, of which he laughed. I replayed this picture in my memory for several days. It was as if I was looking at life through someone else's eyes, yet I know that I was the one who saw this mishap as funny.

Sometimes, even now, I smile at this thought. Anyway, Mr. Ike and I do not see each other as close, but rather, as a team of role models and characters whom the children on our bus have come to depend on when their already challenging disabilities keep them from going forward.

For this reason I call him my very special friend (even if he is only the man in the mirror).

Now it is later in the day, and my family and I went to see our new home. The crew from Lewis modular homes had come earlier in the day to set it on the foundation.

I must say this is a dream come true for all of us. The view from every part of the home provides us with something interesting to look at, whether it is the pond or the field or the road leading to our long driveway. What a thrill it will be to see the landscape change as we will later add more fruit trees, a flower garden, a vegetable garden, and flowering bushes. Time and work will provide such visual beauty that will certainly be worth waiting for.

My thoughts continued as I looked through the sliding glass doors at the picture of a deck to be added on before the fall season arrives, when my focus was interrupted by the sound of Gary's voice complaining of endless problems. And of Mike pondering over what bedroom he wants. Oh well—I can continue to dream about the future even if my boys insist on such verbal chatter.

Chapter 5

Word Confusion

Chapter 5 describes Susie's life and interaction with others. Susie's world is based on the simple life. Everything to her is black and white; and she learns by following orders, rules, and guidance.

Susie has a hard time communicating with others due to word confusion. Susie takes everything very seriously. She doesn't understand when someone may be joking around with her. Susie only understands patterns that lead up to situations. She learns from facial patterns and expressions. The only emotion she truly understands is happiness.

Susie's life is a very simple one. She lives by routine. She has a very hard time responding quickly to a situation and becomes confused very easily. Once she gets to know someone, she will become comfortable with them and will let them into her life, but only to a certain point. She has tried to socialize with her co-workers by going to breakfast or having coffee with them, but it is still very hard for her to do. She has a hard time expressing herself and becoming part of a conversation. If she feels she is being forced to communicate, she becomes nervous and upset and wants to run and hide.

This chapter describes how her boss, Ella, taught her how to communicate. Susie is able to communicate one-on-one much more easily than in a crowd of people. Susie's major fear of socialization is due to the fact that she has a lack of understanding communication. Fears and questions are constantly running through her head. She is continually trying to fit together pieces of the puzzle of the world in which she lives.

As you read this chapter, you will discover that Susie sees the world through the eyes of a child, not a mature adult. She only understands concepts in a book through the pictures, not the words. The words bring too much confusion to her. She has a third-grade reading level.

CHAPTER 5

Here it is the next morning at four o'clock: I was just thinking about all the different things I did, saw, and heard yesterday. This includes the trip to the doctor about Mike's ear, which did not in the least go well for him. And of course, he was mouthing me with many insults, commands, and accusations, especially when Dr. Krause (Mike's pediatrician) told him he needs to see a plastic surgeon about the cyst behind his left ear lobe. That set off an endless flow of nasty words directed at me.

I just do not do well under these types of situations. In fact, I'm not the type to hear words that people say and not take them seriously. When Mike says that I embarrass him, I believe it (although I must admit, I can honestly say I don't know what that means, only that it is not a good thing).

I cannot seem to understand why he feels so upset; I only understand patterns leading up to a situation. Nor do I know how to fix it; instead, I can only repeat the words from the past events, or repeat words and phrases people have suggested over time.

This also fails miserably because my tone or facial expression or even words somehow seem disconnected from the correct emotion.

My solution to most problems is simple, maybe because I only know of one emotion—happy. All other emotions seem to be a nonstop recording: "What did I do?" and "How do I fix it?" "Could it be that folks just don't get it?"

For now, this question and the rest of them can rest in the back of my mind. I would like to redirect my focus to the place where smiles are simple to find and routine is a welcomed blessing.

This, of course, is the bus garage. It will be just a short while before I go there. I just heard Gary's alarm go off, so it is time to turn on the light, make the bed, give Gary a kiss, open Mike's door, and gently say, "Good morning!" Yes, this routine provides me with such joy and soon, a drive to work with good old Charley Pride. (Smiles are coming easy!)

Today, I think I would like to talk about another person at the garage whom I find somehow connected to. This is Garth.

Well, my focus of interest was again interrupted by the sound of Gary's voice. He wanted me to sign for something to do with a credit card advance check statement, I really don't know what. Anyway, he said it was to get money for the house so we would have our utilities put in.

I agreed to sign because it was important. However, the thought of owing money in four-digit figures totaling five thousand dollars scared me, so I informed Gary of this concern; and he laughed, saying that I was funny about such things, and that most people would not be so upset about this amount of money.

Again, I told him that it was an awful lot of money to be responsible for. Gary insisted that he would pay back the money owed on the card, and he further added that I needed to stop being so worried about it. Gary asked me if I wanted to have a nice house, and did I want to have nice things? I then stomped my feet and told him, "I don't care about that; I just care about having things quiet."

As I drove to work, I thought of the conversation we just had and wished I was able just to have said, "I don't like to talk about money this early in the morning." I know I had mentioned this to him many times before; however, for Gary sitting at his desk this early in the day, looking over bills is just a part of his routine and has been for thirty-six years. I did, at this time, feel once again that I had done something wrong. I wish I was able to say the right thing at the right time instead of being slow.

Anyway, I now would like to try to talk about Garth as there is this need to connect the words I write to the person I see and hear every day at work.

I first met Garth in the break room at work. I remember him sitting with other drivers, talking about different issues involving the children on the buses. He spoke of a child with a serious attitude problem, and then, of another whom he felt so bad for due to this child being mistreated at home. I found myself being connected to the stories he told, yet I was not sure why.

At a later date, we were both in a training class together, and it was there when a picture of humor started to develop.

Let me say that laughter (or humor, as it is called on an adult level) does not come easy for me, except on rare occasions; and only when it is on a child's level, or in a cartoon picture.

This was certainly the case on that last evening in the classroom. All the new drivers had this thirty-hour basic-training course to take; and now, at the end of this, was a test. David, then Garth, then I sat at this table conversing back and forth about answers to the questions (this was an open book test). Anyhow, David and Garth were laughing to each other and making jokes, when Garth blustered out an answer to a question, which had me completely in tears with laughter. I thought I was also going to have an accident since I had been laughing so hard.

Although most folks probably would not have thought his answer of "Push the kid off the back of the bus" was anything but funny, I did. I remembered a picture memory of Mr. Ike and a child on our bus named Steven playing a game just a few weeks earlier, joking a lot about pushing Steven off the back of the bus. The rest of the children joined in the fun entertainment with silly facial expressions and added words of jests to the already rowdy situation. So when Garth made that statement, I remembered this and now was able to completely laugh with the fullest understanding.

A few weeks later, David and Garth were in the break room; and I was close by, reading my comic book. I heard David tell Garth that he wished we could all get together again like when we were in class. He suggested getting together for coffee at a nearby restaurant.

As I listened, I was thinking about that class and all the fun we had. I, too, missed our time together. By now my visits to the break room were becoming more and more consistent, for two reasons: One, I was looking for Mr. Ike. And the second reason was because David and Garth had begun to include me in their conversations.

This was awkward for me due to my lack of understanding and also because of speaking in the wrong way. However, I liked the way they would smile at me (it was not scary). I liked the tones of their voices when they said my name. Garth would call me Susie, and David would call me Suz. It had been a long time since anyone had.

Actually, the last time was when I had been in high school. Mr. Odum had called me Susie, and Mr. Trice (a teacher twenty-four years ago and a hall monitor during lunchtime) called me Suz. For me, this was another connected picture memory, a way for me to begin to feel comfortable. David and Garth continued to include me by adding more and more verbal information or questions.

It was, at this time, becoming increasingly difficult to respond in words about what I wanted to say and couldn't say. My way of hiding from this terrible problem was to politely excuse myself, then sit on my bus thinking of all sorts of questions to which I had no answers—everything from "What did Garth mean when he said . . . ?" to "Why do I have such a time with a quick response to a question or comment?"

Day after day, I became more frustrated with this. I began to discuss David and Garth with Mr. Ike. (See, Mr. Ike had worked with and known David for at least ten years). Mr. Ike said that those two would do anything for me, including protect me. He said they would always be looking out for me, like a couple of big brothers.

Well now, another picture of connection was starting to form. I could relate to brothers (I have five). The ones I'm closest to are Tommy and Mike (they are in the middle of the siblings, just like me).

Once this news began to make sense, I shared this with Gary, as I did with everything seen and heard at the garage. Gary encouraged me almost every evening at suppertime to socialize with people, and especially with David and Garth. Although I had many questions as to how to do this since David and Garth were not family, I continued to try.

The first thing I did was talk to Ella. She and I had talked in little bits and pieces about who I am, where I'm from, and my family during those two months of training. Even though I could not forget what she said about not having common sense, I decided she was a sort of mother figure I could trust. I asked her, "How does one socialize?"

She replied, "If I was new in a crowd of people I didn't know but wanted to get to know, I would listen to the conversations around me and wait for an opportunity to hear about some subject I could relate to. Then I would begin to converse."

Well, I thought about this for a long time until, little by little, it made sense. Problem was, I would speak in too much detail of my experiences or sound like a child responding (because answering on an adult level is nothing more than a continuous repeating of words with no meaning). To me, this makes no sense—words without meaning.

After several days of studying a way to break out of this quiet world of mine, I decided that since it was David's idea from a few weeks earlier to have us get the group from class together for coffee, I would ask him to a restaurant to visit with first. For me a one-on-one chat would be much easier than a whole crowd of people. I discussed this with Gary, who agreed, and then later, with David, who also agreed.

David suggested we go to Beamans, and so we did. I found it hard to make eye contact but did begin to talk. I shared with him a little bit about who I am. I told him I only had a third-grade reading level. He didn't seem to believe me.

Of course, what I meant to say and what I did say are two different things. How was I to tell him I only understand the concepts of words in a book through the pictures, mostly from a third grader's reader? How was I to tell him that my way in which I see the world is mostly through the eyes of a child? At that time, I could not; and from the question he asked, "You do? You could have fooled me!" I was not going to make my already uneasy conversation worse by adding more details of myself.

We did continue to talk in bits and pieces of information until, twenty minutes and two cups of coffee later, we parted company, also because it was

Wednesday—cabbage day for me and grocery shopping with his wife, Bonnie, for him.

After returning home, I couldn't wait for Gary to come home so I could tell him about my visit with David. I was filled with an uncomfortableness inside, probably because questions were racing through my head: "Is David going to think I'm a retard?" "Is David going to tell anyone that I have a hard time understanding?" "Is he going to tell others at the garage?" "OH NO, now I'm going to lose my job! Why did I say that to him?"

Fear began to sweep over me, and "What did I do?" "How can I fix it?" repeated over and over again in my head. Back and forth, I paced throughout my house, waiting for Gary to come home for lunch. I needed him to help me sort this out. "Was it a good thing or a bad thing?"

Finally, I heard Gary pull into the driveway. I took a deep sigh and smiled with relief when he walked in. I hugged and kissed him. He was going to help take the pressure of deciding what to do. My handsome—my hero! Repeating word for word what was said, I was assured by him that everything was fine.

Soon after that day, I came to talk to David in little pieces, probably because he was mostly quiet; although sometimes, he would say the dumbest things. Anyway, when talking with David became more and more comfortable, he and Garth would connect with me every day. I felt I was ready for a bigger step in socializing; maybe another coffee setting would be best.

I didn't know what the answer was, and talking with Gary at this time only made it worse. He kept saying, "Stop worrying. Those guys like you. Go on and socialize!" He never stopped to think about all the fears and questions racing through my head, nor did he stop to think that he was not going to be there to help me with the understanding of words or with responding correctly.

Again sorting this out was hard, and I needed more pieces to the puzzle to better understand the concept of the picture. I went to David and asked if he would like to get the gang from class together for coffee. He told me, "That would be nice, Suz."

Again, questions: when, where, who. I thought of all the people who, for one reason or another, connected with me since I became a bus driver.

Now sorting was easy for me: Who was in class? Who taught me to drive? Who were regulars in the break room? "Who smiled at lot? Who talked too much? Who was funny? Who was not? This list of questions in my head continued through the weekend and even into the wee hours of the morning until, at last, the sorting was over. This was done by simply seeing what person or persons showed up most in each category. Now there was a pattern (I always liked and understood them; they made the picture easier to see).

So it was decided, I would ask the following people: David and Garth, of course; George, Sherry, Chuck S., Chuck T., and Michelle. It was, for me, like having three bus trainers, three classmates, and three from the break room.

Next question: where? I had asked those folks at the time of inviting them where they thought would be a nice place to go. Each had their own thoughts on likes and dislikes; however, some pointed out facts or concerns such as "not too far away," "inexpensive but good!"

With those thoughts in mind, I decided that Friendly's would be the best choice. This was sort of exciting for me and yet very scary. The exciting part was that Gary had, over time, encouraged me to socialize by saying, "The people at the bus garage love you; Go and have fun!" The scary part was Gary wasn't going. I had only ever been in these types of situations when someone I was close to and trusted was by my side, and now I had no one—or did I? The thought of David and Garth being like brothers to me once again entered my head, and I began to feel at ease.

CHAPTER 6

MORNING COFFEE—YIKES

Chapter 6 describes Susie's experiences of morning coffee with her co-workers. She was very uncomfortable about going to these as she was not sure of how she would react communicating with her co-workers. She tried to remain calm and relaxed by focusing on good things and repeating over and over the good things that she could think of.

One of the best things to happen to Susie during these morning-coffee times was the fact that she had the opportunity to get to know Garth Wade. She sees Garth as a natural leader, who not only led discussions, but asked many, many personal questions. Susie would avoid certain personal questions such as ones that involved her husband. She would try and change the subject by bringing up her hobbies and things about her life that she is very familiar with. However, this backfired on her because when she brought up her love for old things such as albums, she was laughed at. They didn't understand how valuable these items were to her and how hurt she was when she thought they were laughing at her.

CHAPTER 6

On the morning of this gathering, a smile came to my face as I continued to focus on good things. It was my first time at Friendly's and the first time familiar faces from work were going to sit and chat together. I thought, "This is a good thing." I thought, "These folks smile a lot and make me smile. Yes, this is another good thing."

Over and over, I kept repeating in my mind all the good things I could. Soon, I was completely calm with a more natural smile. While I sat drinking coffee and listening to a variety of stories from the others, I noticed that Garth had become the natural director in that he asked folks several questions about the others' life, you know—where they came from, what they did for a living before coming to the garage, what was their family make up—things like that.

It was quite a few weeks later that I discovered Garth had been a writer for the *Star-Gazette* newspaper. His job was telling human-interest stories. Since I had never read the newspaper (only the comics), I had no way of knowing. Later, it made sense as to why Garth was so good at asking questions.

While conversations continued, Garth came to me next with the question of "Are you married?" I responded, "Yes!" He asked, "How did you meet your husband?" I said nothing because I was more interested in offering others more coffee to make them feel comfortable. As time passed, Garth asked, "Susie, what do you like to do?" This was the topic he had been sharing with others. I answered with great pride, "I love records."

With this statement, I left myself wide open for a flood of comments and questions from the others—questions like, "Do you collect them?" "How much money are they worth?" and comments of "Nobody listens to those anymore!" "What would anyone want with that old junk?"

I felt so hurt inside, but only I knew. The others simply did not know how much old things meant to me, or how music has been my only way of feeling connected in its deepest form. How was I to defend who I was and not feel wounded? I remember blurting out with a smile, "I don't care about the money value; I simply love the old music."

Again the others started with questions and comments. Garth made the first: "What? You don't care about money? Are you crazy?"

This hurt me very much inside because it came from him. The others started laughing and making jokes. I was beginning to feel the hurt surface to the outside of my body when I heard David say something which felt comforting. He said,

"You know, Suz, I have some boxes of old records in my garage. I'll go through them and give you the ones I don't want—that is, if you want them?"

Well that turned my focus back to a positive note. Wow, to have more old music to listen to was simply wonderful.

After this group gathering, I thought about the questions and comments that were made, but mostly of Garth's statement about being crazy. This opened old wounds for me, although he had not a clue. Tears filled my eyes as the pain of being called crazy once again entered my soul. I did not know if talking with Gary would do any good because he always called me that. And every time he does, it hurts in the same way.

So this time, I was truly alone.

Later at suppertime, I shared my morning experience with the family as it was invited into conversation by Gary asking, "So how did it go with your coffee time this morning?" I repeated word for word the conversation from earlier, but I did not tell Gary about Garth's statement and how it made me feel. Both Gary and Mike laughed together about the way in which I handled myself with responses.

Another week went by, and the group met again, this time at Beamans. I went a second time, always with the encouragement of Gary.

This time, I came prepared. I took a family photo album since relating to pictures comes much more natural to me. I showed it to David, Sherry, and Garth.

Sherry seemed to be the only one truly interested in my pictures and the stories that went with each photo as I told some of my stories: first was the time when I had baking classes with neighborhood children, which was abruptly ended by a mother's vicious rumor about me; another, of my first husband injuring my back severely; and still another of my old boyfriend being killed in an explosion.

Garth stated, "Susie, you seem to handle adversity very well!"

Puzzled, I asked, "What does that mean?"

He answered, "That means you handle tragedies well."

This understanding of the word sparked many questions in my thoughts: "What did he mean?" "What tragedies?" I was simply sharing my experiences by connecting the pictures in my album to the chain of events in which they occurred using words. I asked myself, "Was there tragedy in my life? How could anyone say such a thing?"

My stories have meaning—to me, anyway.

Now Garth and the others continued to talk and joke around about different topics. I, on the other hand, felt terribly uncomfortable inside as I looked around at their facial expressions. I could not understand. More questions entered my already overloaded thoughts: Did these people not believe me? Did these people not care about the happy endings to each story? Was I supposed to feel bad? Had I done something wrong? I'm feeling uncomfortable; what do I do?

At this time, a driver named Renny entered the room to join the crowd in conversation. He was invited by me at an earlier date, to help me enter into this world of socialization. When I asked him, I remember thinking of what Ella had said about listening for a subject I could relate to. I remember Gary's insistence on socializing, and I remembered my manners (don't be rude!). I certainly did not wish to hurt Renny's feelings by not asking him to join us when others were talking with excitement about the coffee group.

Renny is a smart man who is reserved in facial expression (probably from his days in the service—the Air Force, I think?). He is respected by many folks but disliked by others at the garage. Still he is a co-worker and a human being, who is to be treated politely. Renny was now settled in a seat and joining in conversation.

It wasn't long before his focus was on me. He was much like Garth in that he asked me lots of questions. I did the best I could in giving answers that were honest (this was a rule I learned as a child) yet short and simple. It was difficult at times, but I made it through the long time period (forty-two minutes, to be exact) without being rude (more rules I learned as a child).

I found myself and Renny soon sitting alone as the others had left the restaurant, and my focus was only on "not breaking the rules of manners." I looked at my watch and realized it was after 11:00 a.m. I had to go home to meet Gary for lunch. I said "thank you" and "goodbye" to Renny.

After this coffee group, I was not sure I could ever try another. I got in my car and drove home thinking over and over of questions I had no answers to, but mostly, of Garth's statement about adversity. I had to know what the understanding was as to why he said it. People say things with meaning, don't they? If they don't, why do they say them?

I did wish that Gary could have been there. He was so good at conversations. He could explain some things to me easy, and still others he could not; but just having him close to me was all I needed to make my fears go away. He is, after all, my friend, my husband—my hero.

All the wishing in the world would not ease the painful reality that he was not able to join me on this day. I was on my own in a foreign country, unable to understand the language. All I could do was repeat my experiences and follow the rules, yet never really connecting to others.

Gary's whole idea about socializing was, to me, making no sense; and the words he had been expressing to me over a period of time were racing through my head: "Honey, I want you to make friends." "I'm worried about you being alone after I'm gone!" "I think you found a home at the bus garage!"

These statements were not connecting with any picture of understanding. However, I was only good at one thing: doing what I'm told. And today, I did just that—but I did not have Gary there during the coffee time to tell me what to do and what to say.

Throughout the rest of my morning at home, I decided to listen to my records since my eyes caught their attention on the way through the dining room. In no time, I began joining in words of the songs being played. I was beginning to feel happy, and I settled down from my early morning journey. Yes, music gave meaning to me. It provides security, especially good ole Charley Pride (I had now been listening to him on the record player), followed by Kitty Wells, Waylon Jennings, and the Statler Brothers, all in that order—the same order my dad listened to them when I was a child.

The records were old and warped, but they played without a skip, and the words and melody were simple. These artists told a story (I like picture book stories). I could understand because they used their words in the song to compose a picture; the music provides the feeling in its deepest form.

I had now become so happy and was ready for a change. I decided to listen to the children's records. Yes, children's music provides me with a constant repeating of silly words with simple melodies of music. I was truly so comfortable in my world of songs and dance.

A short time later, I was driving back to work (continuing my good feelings by listening to the cassette of Charley Pride in my car). As I pulled in the parking lot, I saw David's van. This reminded me of what he had said: "I have boxes of old records in my garage."

I thought, no, I need to mind my manners and not be greedy or impatient. I simply won't ask him about the records. I will smile and wave instead.

I was so happy. I could hardly wait for the afternoon bus run. The children on my bus made sense to me. I understood them, and they understood me. We had so much fun together.

Later this day, during suppertime, Gary and Mike and I were talking about our day's events. I shared another word-for-word repeat of my coffee chat, followed by questions directed to Gary to help me better understand: "Why would Garth say I handle adversity well?"

Gary and Mike answered together, "You do!"

The only response that came to my mind was "If people think that life is perfect, then that is just stupid!"

Gary laughed and said, "Honey, the way you smile and accept life as it happens is stupid!"

Now I was getting myself ready to fight back, to defend my beliefs in the only way I knew how. I spoke in a much louder voice (this I learned from listening to Gary), saying, "Well, if living in a perfect world is all folks want to see, then they're stupid! Perfect people make me sick! I don't ever want to be perfect, it's not normal."

After several minutes of a chain reaction of comments toward perfect people, I started to cry. Gary and Mike did not seem to know why. Gary said with a nasty tone, "What the hell is the matter now?"

I muttered, "I hate the people at the bus garage. Why do I have to socialize anyway?"

At that time, no matter what Gary or Mike said, it was clear to me that again, I had no understanding. What I did know was that earlier, my music and the children filled my heart with songs of joy, but I was now under the attack of words with no meaning.

Day after day, the music in my car during trips to and from work, the smiles from co-workers, the bus, and the children were the only simple routine parts in my life that made sense. Still I knew Gary and Mike loved me, and this made sense. Their constant concerns about me socializing did not. How am I going to begin to get to know people? How were they going to get to know me?

I liked it better when all I did was smile and say small polite words. Gary did not want my lack of understanding communication to get in the way of my job. Still he would send me back to yet another coffee chat. I knew he was looking at Garth and David as my big brothers.

I liked Garth. He made me laugh, and I liked the way he called my name "Susie" always with a cheerful tone. I liked David also. He was quiet, says little, and smiles a lot at people. But they were not my brothers, and they knew hardly anything about me.

My way of getting to know people is slow and simple—like wandering close to the picnic table and listening. Like the time Garth, George, Renny, Mr. Ike, Chuck, Lou, and others were talking among themselves, and I heard Garth say, "When my wife gets a migraine, even the deer tiptoe past the house."

This cracked me up because all I could think of was the Christmas cartoon I had seen once of the deer tiptoeing past Santa's workshop with silly expressions on their faces.

Another time, I was listening to Garth over the radio from my bus telling Donna (the dispatch lady), "I'll be there in eighty-seven and a half seconds." Again this cracked me up, "eighty-seven and a half seconds."

My way of socializing was sending little notes, like "Have a nice Turkey Day" or a card that says, "I care." Even making candy to share with others at the garage was a way of expressing myself. Also talking about the little things in my life that make me happy, and finally, playing on a child's level, was certainly my style of socializing.

Gary did not understand this.

Instead I was attending yet a third attempt at the coffee chat. This time, it would prove to be the worst. We went to Beamans. There was Garth, David, and George. I was the only girl. I wondered why Sherry didn't come.

Although we were in a public place, the thought of the three of them and I together made me uncomfortable inside. They only saw my smile on the outside. (My grandma always said, "Smile and the world smiles back; frown and you frown alone.")

I began to think about Gary. I didn't want him to be mad, but I really wanted to go home.

David was smiling, as always. Garth was joking, and George was laughing. I just sat there smiling and thinking. Soon the waitress came. David began to say something to her about having his baby.

With this, my eyes widened with fear. Garth and George were adding words to David's chat with the waitress then took notice to me as I sat there in complete disbelief as to what I had just heard. David now leaned over and hugged me, saying, "I'm just kidding, Suz." Garth and George were laughing. I didn't know why, and I was not happy and didn't understand why David hugged me. What was going on? Did these people want me to have their baby?

The whole situation was making me sick. I sat there frozen in my seat, unable to sort out the words that had been spoken. I was gasping for my breath, then statements of rules flooded my mind: "Respect your elders," "Be polite," "Don't yell," "Don't scream," "Close your mouth," "Take your hand away from your mouth," "Don't fidget," "Stop shaking," "Don't cry," "Stop looking so worried," "Smile, smile, smile."

By this time my smile was slightly crooked, but somehow, I managed to continue to sit in a natural-looking position. Inside, I was stiff. The fellows were talking about different things; and my eyes were roaming about, looking at their faces with quick glances, then at the table, where I spotted my coffee cup. I quickly grabbed my cup and started drinking. The warm drink made my inside feel calmer.

Still with a half smile, I began thinking of Gary. Oh, how I wished he was here. I was listening to the conversation, but only in bits and pieces. I heard someone say that Garth had worked at the *Star-Gazette*. This caught my attention. I looked at him and then asked, "You worked for the newspaper?"

Garth said, "You didn't know that?" George added, "Yeah, he worked for years at the *Star-Gazette*."

I answered Garth by saying, "No." I said, "What did you do?"

Garth said, "I wrote human-interest stories. I am a local celebrity." David was laughing, and Garth was laughing.

I asked, "What is human interest?"

Garth said, "You know—I wrote about people."

I didn't understand. "What people?" I asked.

George said, "People and the different things that happen to them."

Still very much lost, I asked, "Like what?"

Garth answered, "The tragedies in their life, the good things in their life, stuff like that."

I thought to myself, "There is that word again: *tragedies*."

I also thought about the good things. I thought about Gary and I, and about my wedding day. This put a smile on my face. The fellows were laughing, and Garth asked, "Susie, you never read my article?"

I replied, "I never read the paper."

Again, the fellows were laughing—only this time, louder and longer. I heard David say, "Suz, you never read the paper? How come?"

I said, "I told you before, I only have a third-grade reading level."

Then Garth added, "How did you come this far?"

I didn't know what he meant. George said, "Do you even know what a newspaper is?" Again, they laughed.

I spoke very proudly, saying, "Yes, my handsome reads it to me every Sunday before church."

Everyone spoke together saying, "Ohhhh." I looked at George and then asked, "Do you want to see a picture of him?" I then quickly pulled out my wallet and showed everyone with pride my family, pointing out my handsome husband and my handsome son.

I asked George if he had picture of his wife. He did not. I asked, "How did you meet your wife?" George began to tell the story, and soon, I asked David, then Garth. What I did not know was that they were going to ask me the same question. I was just happy that they were not laughing at me anymore, and that just seeing the picture of Gary made me feel as if he were close, and I was not afraid anymore.

Now the time came. Garth asked, "Susie, how did you meet your handsome?" Then the others were chuckling.

I said nothing. I just sat there in complete silence. George was laughing, saying it must be pretty bad. Garth said, "Come on, it's only fair. You asked us."

I still sat there saying nothing. My mind was a complete blank.

Garth said, "Susie, you got us curious now. Tell us how you met your husband."

Then David said, "She doesn't want us to know because it is none of our business, right, Suz?"

I said, "Yes—I mean, no. I mean, I got to go now."

The drive home seemed so long. I was crying, barely able to see ahead. Thoughts raced in my head again like a movie being played over but in slow motion: The laughing, the faces, the words, the tones, the pictures of Gary and Mike. What had I done? How do I fix it? I don't like feeling this way.

Now home, I ran to my bed and grabbed my blankies, sobbing harder and harder. I didn't want to go anymore to these stupid coffee chats. My senses were completely overloaded. I just wrapped myself tight in my blankets with my blankies to my face and fell asleep.

When I woke up, I heard Gary in the bathroom. He had come home for lunch. I went over to him and hugged him so tight, saying, "I love you, handsomest."

Gary kissed me then started grumbling about how the tenant at the Hudson Street apartment had screwed him out of a month and a half's rent, further adding about chasing after customers for money and all the running around he had to do before the day was over. While making his lunch, he complained more about the little things in the kitchen that were out of place. "Honey, where is my spoon?" "I can't find my spoon. It's not in the drawer." "What moron took it?"

I looked in the dishwasher and there it was. He said, "What the hell is it doing in there?" I told him I put it there by accident. I told him, "I'm sorry!"

He now took his lunch in the living room, sat in his chair, and turned on the television, grumbling more about the TV controllers not working right.

He wanted to see where the stock market was, since he has investments in the market. I helped him get the program he wanted. Now focused on the television, he grumbled some more. "Son of a bitch, the damn market is down!" "I'm gonna lose my ass." Soon he turned it off and asked me how my morning went.

I told him, "I decided no more coffee chat for me. That's it. I don't care if I have friends or not."

Gary's response was loud and mean: "What the hell did you do now?"

I was now overloaded again. I began screaming, repeating words, statements, and comments he had made in the past.

He grabbed his coat, raced out the door yelling, "You're crazy. I can't take this anymore."

I continued screaming, saying, "I can't take this anymore. You're crazy!" I remember slamming the door to the kitchen and throwing a dish towel on the floor, then stomping my feet on the way to the living room, where I sat down and began to cry, repeating, "I'm crazy, I'm crazy, I'm crazy." Oh how, I wish I wasn't.

Rocking back and forth, crying, my eyes caught my bus driver's ID tag setting on the coffee table. Then I looked at the clock. In twenty minutes or so, I have to go to work. I went into the bathroom and splashed water on my face, combed my hair, then grabbed my keys, wallet, ID tag, and Scooby Doo Van (a bag filled with toys for the children on the bus) and was driving to work. Good ole Charley Pride calmed my senses.

At work, I looked around for any vehicle that looked familiar. I saw David's van, Sherry's car, and a bus drive past me before I entered the parking lot. I smiled and waved to that person. Inside my car, I was safe from words or up-close expressions. How I loved the security of my bus and the children. Yes, it is these little simple things that make me happy.

Later at the supper table, the discussion was about Mike and an interim report that came in the mail. Gary was loud and nasty with accusations toward Mike about his laziness. He went on further to say that Mike's attitude was just like Mike's dad's.

Throughout the constant attack of words directed at Mike, I repeated over and over to Gary about how this was not Mike's fault. That it was, in fact, Gary himself who had not been there for him. I pointed out, "You are always so busy making yourself happy with your needs and wants, you simply do not see that Mike and I need your help."

Gary insisted, "You got to have money. I can't pay the bills without money, you moron!"

I said, "Honey, Mike and I need a routine and structure every day, and part of that routine is having you spend time with each of us with our needs and wants. You can't be so selfish all the time."

Well, Gary clearly was not going to see things differently. He snapped at me, saying, "I'm not selfish. I put food on the table, a roof over your head, and clothes on your back. I don't go out at night." As he continued to give us a list of what he does for us, I looked at Mike and smiled, telling him, "I understand."

Soon, it was later in the evening, and Gary and I were watching the television when Gary asked me about my morning and why I didn't want to go to the coffee thing anymore.

I told him about what was said. He laughed, and now Mike came into the room to hang up the phone. Gary told Mike about my morning: what David and the waitress said, what Garth said, what George said. Then the two of them were laughing together.

I felt hurt inside and started to cry. Mike said, "It's okay, Mommy, they were only kidding. David and Garth pick on you because they like you."

I cried anyway because I didn't understand about words with no meaning, about laughing at others, about answering questions, about this stupid socialization thing. I decided to go to bed.

CHAPTER 7

FRIENDSHIP

Chapter 7 describes Susie's relationships with the students on her bus and also those whom she works with. It is very hard for Susie to become close to someone, and yet she was able to open up her heart and mind to become friends with the children on her bus and with two of her co-workers, along with some teachers when she was in high school.

This chapter describes how Susie met a little girl on her bus who had very similar characteristics to her own. When she saw this little girl, or the reactions this little girl had, it reminded her of her own childhood and the situations she was in. This chapter also deals with Susie trying to understand the different types of relationships between boys and girls. She has a very hard time understanding the concept of boyfriend/girlfriend.

Susie also had to face a good friend of hers leaving the bus garage for a different job. She couldn't understand why her friend was leaving when she was so happy working there. She didn't understand why he would want to better himself with a position working for a congressman. She didn't understand the need to better himself, to fulfill his life in a position with more prestige than he had now. Susie was very upset with this and had a very hard time dealing with it and understanding what work would be like without her friend there.

CHAPTER 7

When I lay down at night, I thought of Jesus, and I thanked him for those wonderful children on my bus that day. As I continue to reflect back on my first year at the bus garage, I am finding that many changes took place—some forced, some of circumstances, and some which came truly natural (like where my inner self yearned to be, which was connecting with those children on my bus).

Playing with the children was easy; the simple games from the toys I brought and the repeating of commercials or television theme songs provided a natural communication throughout our trips. Gently reminding them of the rules of manners and safety also created a natural smoothness for me.

Still there was one child I seemed to be drawn to in an almost haunting unspoken way. This was Sandra. She is autistic.

At first, when I worked with the children, she seemed shy. She would put her head down or look the other way when I spoke to her (always soft and with a smile). When she did this, a picture memory of me as a child would surface in an eerie way. I told myself, she just needs time to get to know me in much the same way as I do in new situations. Every day, I would smile and softly speak to her, "Good morning," "Have a nice day," "Have a good night"; and every day, she would turn her head, never looking at my face.

Again, this sent a chill through my inside as a memory of me would appear in my thoughts.

Once in a while, I quite by accident would place my hand on her shoulder, thinking it was the back of her seat, as I was discussing a problem of rules to the child sitting in the seat behind her. At those times, she would jerk her head, then look into my eyes with fear.

Again, my mind replayed times when I, too, reacted in the same manner. I just told myself not to worry; she is just having a hard time.

Christmas vacation was in a few days. The joys of this were endless for the children. However, for me, not seeing them would prove to be hard. I did so enjoy their company.

Then just before the holiday break, Mr. Ike and I were told that Sandra had broken her ankle and would not ride until further notice. I kept wondering about her during vacation—you know, how she was doing? But more oddly, I found myself thinking about when I had broken bones and other injuries, and asking, "I wonder if Sandra felt pain?" I knew I never did. Why, then, would I even be curious about whether or not she did? This made no sense.

I remained busy during our time off with small projects that Gary needed done, spending time with Mike, and playing with my toys I bought from the hundred dollars Gary's mom had given me as a present. However, I couldn't shake this connection with Sandra; what was this about? I decided that, no matter what, I'm not going to think about her anymore. I had to break free from this haunting feeling that kept bugging me. It wasn't making sense.

After we returned from what seemed to be a lengthy absence from work, my thoughts were filled with happiness. The routine had returned: Garth was again calling out my name, "Susie" (with a cheerful voice). David was smiling. Alta was standing in the hallways (as always). Ella was in her office. The bus was parked in the same place, and the children were back riding. Oh, how I had missed these simple things in my life.

I did not, however, miss Sandra as much, and I quickly allowed someone else to sit in her seat. Soon, her memory would be temporarily buried, and I would not have to feel uncomfortable about it.

Seeing, listening, and playing with the children certainly provided good feelings. Even Mr. Ike's comment about comparing Gary and I to Tinkerbell and the Grinch (this was Gary) was accepted as good. Since many folks over the years have often taken notice of my fairylike ways (putting my arms up like a bird and smiling, especially when I'm happy), I did not mind this statement at all.

Some changes were about to take place during those first few weeks of New Year 2001. Mr. Ike and I were told we were going to have a new student riding on our bus. I was pleased at first. However, this was to be a very difficult transition for me. There was a girl already riding on the bus who was sometimes a challenge, not because she did bad things, but more because of what she talked about.

She was a teenager who always let us know how pretty she is and that boys liked this about her. She would let us know about her dates with boys, sometimes trying to inform us of every detail. Also, she would tell us about how other girls were jealous of her. This would include the new girl who was joining us.

Now for me, this whole understanding of wanting boys, being a teenager, and jealousy was certainly something I did not have a true picture of. Yes, I had been a teenager. Yes, had liked boys (to a point). Yes, I knew, sort of, what jealousy was. But no, I didn't have any idea what *popular* meant.

In listening to the girls over time about this teenager thing, I remembered back to when I was a teenager. Although I stood mostly against the wall with my head down during those years in high school, I could hear conversations from the others. Some would talk about being on the sports team; others would talk about the latest music, clothes, movies, or food; and still others would talk about boys' butts or girls' boobs—all of which, then and today, made little to no sense to me.

What I wanted was a friend—just one friend—who smiled and was not going to laugh at me, pick on me, make faces that were scary, or talk too much.

I found just such a person, two to be exact: these were Mr. Odum and Mr. Trice, of whom I spoke of earlier. They are still my friends after twenty-four years (people I trust). I thought of how they accepted me just as I was and who I became.

With this in mind, I was able to work better with those girls on my bus. With a soft smile, gentle words, and rules of manners or safety, the girls allowed my lack of understanding of their interests to be tolerated. Soon, the uneasiness of conversation became comfortable and respected.

Another change that took place was to be the hardest of all. This was when I went to see Ella about something (I can't remember what it was), but at the end of this talk, she told me that Garth was leaving.

I was devastated! How could this happen? Why was he leaving?

Ella told me he was going to work with a congressman. This made no sense to me. Why would he even think about working for someone else? Wasn't he happy at the bus garage? I was happy he was here as a driver and my friend.

As these questions raced in my head, my eyes took notice of him outside the office window. I politely excused myself from Ella's company and then hurried to catch up with Garth. I hugged him and then gently told him, "I heard you are leaving."

He said, "Yeah, but I can't talk to you right now. George and the others are meeting for breakfast." I said, "When is your last day?" He said, "Friday." A lump was in my throat. This was two days away. I spoke with a crack in my voice, "Oh!"

Then I slowly walked to my car, looking over my shoulder at him and crying. I thought to myself how much I was going to miss him. Still, there was so much I wanted to ask him, so much I wanted to tell him. I thought about the motorcycle ride he promised to take me on in the spring. I still had my helmet in the back of my car. I thought about his promise to come to my anniversary picnic party in June. I did so want him to meet my handsome and my handsome son. Was he going to come? He promised. He has to come. People mean what they say, don't they? I felt so sick when I got to my car. Then I cried harder.

The drive home was terribly long, and it was hard to see the road. I had to pull over twice to wipe my eyes. Once home, I paced rapidly back and forth from the living room to the dining room, talking to myself out loud. "This is my fault. If only I wasn't so scared of conversation, I would have known about this sooner instead of now with two days left. I hate being slow!" "I can't understand why anyone would want to leave the bus garage!" "I will never see him again." I began to cry again and stomp my feet. "Why? Why? Why?" This makes no sense. Tears flooded my eyes as I continued to stomp my feet and pace the floor, waving my arms up and down and saying, "No! No! This can't be happening!" "I have to know why."

Just then, as I waved my arms, my hand flew down, hitting the telephone. I stopped all motion and stared at it a few moments and wiped my eyes. I thought, "What was I to do? Who was I to call?"

My eyes were focused on that phone, but the complete understanding was not registering any sense. I remember closing my eyes so tight and tightening my hands into a fist, swallowing hard, and then a picture memory of Garth at the garage entered my mind. I opened my eyes only to find them again frozen on the phone. Then the understanding started to surface. Call Garth and ask him, duh!

I looked up his number in the drivers' directory, which was given out each year. I called his house, completely forgetting about him going to breakfast. Mrs. Garth answered.

I explained who I was and how I had come to call. She sounded so nice, but I had a very difficult time communicating comfortably. She made reference to where Garth might have gone and when he might return. She further added that David might know, although she wasn't sure if he had gone too. I asked if she had David's number. She sweetly gave it to me and told me she would let Garth know that I called.

Now I had to keep trying to make sense out of this situation, so I called David. There was no answer. I left a message on the machine and hung up. I kept replaying the words Mrs. Garth said in my mind, but only some had understanding for me. The rest did not. I remembered her saying she thought perhaps he may have gone to Maple Lawn. This put a direction in which to follow for finding answers. I got in my car and drove quickly to this restaurant as time was becoming an issue because it was now 9:40 AM and I had spoken to Garth one hour and ten minutes earlier.

When I got there, I saw no familiar vehicles (of course, the only one I knew was David's van, and it was not there). I went inside and went looking for anyone from the garage. There was no one. All I saw were scary faces looking at me and smiling. I walked to my car crying. People inside knew him as a celebrity. I knew him as Garth, the bus driver who was leaving; didn't they care? Didn't they know he was going away?

As I drove home, my head felt numb, my body felt weak, and my inside empty.

Now home, my focus was on my chores. I had cabbage to shred, garbage to pull, and cat boxes to clean, all of which seemed meaningless. Soon, the phone rang. It was David. I had forgotten until then that I left a message.

I told him I just found out about Garth and how this was upsetting to me. David very softly said, "I'm sad about him leaving too, Suz. But people come and go all the time. That's part of life." By this time, the words he spoke and the tone in which he said them provided me with a more comfortable way of accepting this—even though there was not a complete understanding.

Later that evening at the supper table, I told Gary the news I heard earlier in the day. I asked him, "What is a congressman?"

Gary laughed and proceeded to tell me in great length of who they are and what they do. I told him, "So it's someone who sits at a desk and does nothing except run his mouth."

Gary laughed some more and said, "Yeah, that's about it."

I asked, "Then why would anyone want to go to a job where all they do is talk?

He said, "For the money!"

I said, "Who cares about money? People should have a job they enjoy! Mrs. Garth said he liked being a bus driver, and he was going to miss the children."

Gary kept insisting that I didn't understand about such things as money and positions to better oneself. I kept insisting that if one likes their job, what could be better?

All the talk about congressmen, money, or happiness was not going to change the fact that Garth was leaving. Remembering David's words from our phone conversation earlier in the day was not going to change the fact that I still did not talk with Garth in person. Even if I did, I was not sure I would have known what to say because I am slow, and there simply was not time to get into a lengthy conversation about what I wanted to say and couldn't.

Remembering the additional words from the phone call with David when he said I'll still see Garth on most weekends provided me with a new sense of security. I could always ask David how he is doing and maybe see him once in a while.

That night, my final words to Garth came in the form of a note, with the hope that he would want to keep in touch with me. I told him how I enjoyed his company and hoped we would remain friends. I placed the note on his seat on his bus (number 290).

On the following Monday, I came to work with the thought that maybe, just maybe, he would be there. Perhaps it was just a bad dream last week, or perhaps he changed his mind.

But it was not the case. I had been listening for him to call my name, "Susie." All I heard was the engines of the buses. I found myself looking for him, walking to his bus.

I had always liked the way he dressed because it reminded me of my most respected cartoon character, Professor Ludwig Von Drake. Von Drake appeared once in a Donald Duck cartoon as a professor observing Donald's parenting abilities with his nephews, Huey, Dewey, and Louie. During one scene, Donald is trying to coach his nephews on baseball. Von Drake is close by watching and taking notes. Von Drake is dressed in a sweatshirt, a baseball cap, and a landyard around his neck. My friend, Garth, wore this outfit the same way, taking me to fond picture memories as a child during the time when my family watched Disney cartoons.

I did not, however, see the joy in the memory of Garth on this day. Instead, there were only clouds of smoke from the exhaust pipes of the buses. I felt now this was no dream. This was reality, and I hurt inside. Again, I felt a lump in my throat, and my chest felt tight. I now put my hand to my chest as it hurt badly. Then my fingers grabbed the lanyard around my neck. This was the one Garth had given me back in October to put my bus driver's ID tag on. A small smile came to my mouth and a tear to my eye. I hung on to this moment throughout the rest of the day as this gave me a sense of joy and hope through which I could be somewhat comfortable in accepting this change.

From that day on, I have made it a point to look for David's vehicle in the parking lot, David's bus (Number 277) passing my bus on the way to transporting children; and I made sure I saw him even though he was not aware of me doing it. The thought of having him leave entered my mind as well, and that would be more than I could bear since there is an unspoken trust with him, of which he has no clue. I asked him once, "Are you going to leave the bus garage?" He said, "No, Suz, I don't plan on going anywhere for quite a while."

Shortly after that, I found another whom I could lean on. This was George, and although I had not spoken much to him other than regular polite words of everyday conversation, he later would become my good friend as well. I knew that Garth, David, and George were very good friends, both at work and off. I also knew that I needed a great deal of guidance for such things as answers to my questions and a big brother role model I could simply stand close to when I felt afraid or lonely. I had once asked George if he could be my big brother since Garth was no longer there. George put his arm around my shoulder, chuckled, and said, "Sure, I'll be your big brother." Now keep in mind, George had no idea how much touch from another man besides my handsome or my son bothered me, nor did he know I was not able to understand his laughing (was it a good thing or a bad thing?). Still I told George, "Thank you!" and I gradually built up a certain kind of respect and trust.

As the changes at the bus garage were slow and sometimes painful, nothing prepared me for what was about to happen as the doors from my past opened up with truths about my family, my experiences, my friends, and me—truths that are to be written with unbelievable pain and yet a new beginning for an inner peace I have waited a lifetime (thirty-nine years) to find.

Before I begin, let me again remind you that, as I said in the earlier part of my writings, there is no particular order of a beginning or an end, but a continuous series of visual memories from my experiences with people and the selfish things they say and do in this world that has made little to no sense to me until now. Many questions I have had will now have answers, although brand new ones will follow with none—the private lifelong battle that is just a part of being Susie.

Soon after the adjustment of losing a friend and adding a friend, this brought a thought to mind of a child whom I had not seen in a while. It happened to be Sandra. Although I decided not to focus on her because of an unspoken connection that kept haunting me, I realized that eight weeks had gone by since she broke her ankle, and soon, she would be riding again. However, I was no longer bothered with answering the questions I had about her. Instead, the thoughts were more driven to filling this void of having the missing child from my bus return.

I did so very much want to have her feel the joys and security I had with the children every day. Their fun was simple and pure. I found myself preparing for her return in many ways, and always with a deep sense of excitement, which the others on board had only caught small glimpses of. I moved her name tag over the best seat available on the bus. I informed the other children not to sit in her seat as she would be returning soon. I had even gotten information about autism from Ella as I needed to find a way to talk to Sandra.

CHAPTER 8

AUTISM

Chapter 8 describes Susie's discovery of the word *autism* and who she really is. All of Susie's life, she realized that she was different from others around her, but she never knew exactly why until one day, when Ella gave her some papers to read. The information was to help Susie learn to understand the needs of one of her special children on the bus. However, not only did this occur, but Susie also discovered who she is and why she is so different from anyone else; and it was quite simple and complex at the same time. It is due to the word *autism*.

Susie did extensive research on the subject of autism to see if it truly is what was wrong with her. Not only did she do research in the library, but she contacted her grandfather and friends of the family to ask them questions about her earlier years. The more stories she heard, the more she realized that yes, indeed, she does have autism.

At first, this scared her because she didn't want to believe it. She didn't want to feel as though she were different from others around her. She needed more and more evidence, so she continued to look for facts about it, to see if she did have it.

Susie remembered a visit with the doctor and how her parents were in denial that Susie had autism. Her father stated that his daughter just doesn't want to grow up, and yet her mother believed it was because Susan was so stubborn. After going over and over everything in her mind, Susie finally believed that yes, she does have autism; and now she knew what was wrong with her.

CHAPTER 8

I had heard of autism only once before, back when I was sixteen, from the psychiatrist who was working with me during a hospital stay for inappropriate behaviors; and my parents did not believe in such nonsense. However, this was the second time I had the word before me and the understanding of which I did not want to hear.

I remember reading over the papers Ella had given me a couple months earlier and had decided that they were an absolute assortment of words that made no sense.

Here, two months later, I found myself again attempting to understand how to communicate with Sandra through those pages with words that seemed to be of meaningless information; then I stood up from my chair, staring at the wall, and a chill of an almost unbearable fear swept over my body; and my fingers flung the papers on the floor. I began sweating, then my breathing became fast and heavy. Why was I having a panic attack? This made no sense. I sat down, swallowing hard, thinking to myself, why am I afraid? Why can't I understand the meaning of words I read? Why was a picture of Sandra flashing in my head? What was the connection?

My eyes became full of tears; and I looked up at the pictures on the wall of my mom, my brothers, my sister, my grandparents, my dad, then to the one of Gary and me.

That's it. Gary. He could explain what was wrong, I think? Yes—he could. He always tried anyway. After all, he read the newspaper to me, he explained the words in the CDL driver's manual to prepare me for the written test, and he also told me about the people I met on my journeys in life. Now I didn't need to be worried anymore. I would just wait until he came home later in the day after my bus run, when he could read those papers and help me understand.

During my afternoon trip with the children, I thought very little about what had happened earlier; the game punch car absorbed much of my attention, and a chat with Mr. Ike also made the time pass quickly.

When I got home, my focus was almost immediately turned back to those papers. I could hardly wait to have Gary come home so he could explain what they meant. Finally, after my chores of closing the blinds, turning on the lights, setting the table, cooking the liver, and letting the dogs inside from the kennels, I heard Gary pull into the driveway.

He came into the house in a pretty good mood, but I did have to wait for his chores to be done before talking to him—you know, like, he has to put his stuff on his desk, change his clothes, go to the bathroom, start dinner, grab a beer, and then sit down for a few minutes.

Well, I couldn't wait anymore. I said, "Honey, would you please read these papers and tell me what they mean?" He said, "Well, what in the hell are they?" I said, "They are papers about some learning disability called autism, and I got them from Ella to help me better understand how to talk to a girl on my bus, but I don't think they make any sense." Gary laughed and said, "That's my wife—always lost." I insisted that he stop making jokes about me being slow and just read the papers.

I sat in my chair watching him read, then he looked up at me smiling and said, "Are you sure they aren't talking about you?"

Puzzled, I said, "What?"

He said, "This problem is what you got!"

I was starting to get upset because Gary is always joking, and I demanded he stop his nonsense and help me because this is important to me. He replied, "I'm not joking, honey. This is what's wrong with you. You have a communication problem."

I raised my voice saying, "I do not!"

Now Mike had come out of his room and asked, "What's going on?" Gary said, "Mike, we know what's wrong with your mother. She's autistic."

I stood up, stomped my foot on the floor and screamed, "I am not!"

Gary said again, "Honey, yes you are. From what I just read, you are definitely autistic." I began to cry.

Then I heard Mike ask Gary if he could read the papers. I sat down and waited for Mike to get done reading. He had said nothing while looking at those pages, but he did raise his eyebrows and sort of looked sad. I asked him, "Well, Gary's wrong, isn't he?" Mike said, "I don't know, Mommy." It sounds like you might be."

Then Gary yelled from the kitchen, "See, I told you. Even your own kid agrees."

I screamed out the word *no* several times, crying and rocking back and forth in my chair. Gary now insisted that I calm down as my volume was making a whistling sound in his hearing aid.

I dropped my head, putting my hands over my face, sobbing hard; thoughts raced in my head of questions I had no answers to: "What is everyone talking about?" "What is this autism?" "Is Gary just plain lying to me?" "How come Mike is wondering about it?" "Is this true or false?" "Is it good or bad?" "What did I do?" "How do I fix it?" "Why do I feel so awful; I just wanted to talk with Sandra?"

Mike had come over to me and hugged me tight, saying, "It's okay, Mommy. We still love you."

I lifted my head muttering, "It's not true."

Then my eyes took notice of the photos on the wall. First was my mom. I stared at it for several minutes thinking she would know the answers, but she had died in 1991 of the cancer. I inhaled deeply and shifted now to the other photos, the ones of my brothers and sister, my grandpa and grandma. With another deep breath, I thought if Grandma had not taken a trip to heaven, I could have asked her, especially since she had a calming way of explaining things so I could understand.

Just then, Gary called us out to the supper table.

I decided I needed more information and facts before I was going to let him trick me again. I smiled at him and said, "I'm perfectly normal, and if you don't believe me, just ask my family."

Gary laughed hard and loud, saying, "Your family is a bunch of goddamn closet cases. What do they know about anything?"

I insisted that my family was just fine; and that if I had any such problem as this autism, they would have helped me.

Gary responded, "Sweetie, that's what you have, and that's why they treated you like shit."

I laughed, saying, "Well, my family loves me, and I don't have any problems."

Gary laughed, saying, "Honey, that's why I love you—because you're slow." He smiled, patted me on my shoulder, nodded his head, adding, "I'm afraid, it is true."

A few days later, I walked to the library to find information about this autism so I could prove to Gary it wasn't so. I had found only three books on the subject, all written by the same lady, "Donna Williams."

When I returned home, I was proud that Gary was now going to see without a doubt that he was wrong. Then a thought of fear entered my head: "What if Gary reads them and finds out he is wrong and insists otherwise since he prides himself on being right?" I stared at the books for a while. I really didn't know how I was going to find out facts about the subject since I never read a book without pictures, graphs, drawings, or any visual aids to guide me through the words. I thought, well, he can read them; and once he does, I'm sure he will realize he doesn't know what he's talking about.

I made coffee and walked through the dining room. My eyes caught the stack of books on the table. I picked up the top one, "Nobody Nowhere." I sat down and began to read the first three pages. As I read, I thought, this woman is on drugs. This has nothing to do with me.

I put it down, drank my coffee, and found myself returning to the book. I read those first three pages again, and a chill went in my spine. I remembered when I too had similar experiences.

I read more and more. I started to remember pieces of my childhood. I started thinking of being slapped for the same things Donna had been. I began breathing harder and told myself, "Look, it's not true about this autism stuff. This is just normal behavior of children; and besides, the librarian said, 'Donna is a severe autistic.'" I'm normal because that's what people have told me for years. Anyway, Donna had parents that smoked, drank, and swore. I didn't. Donna was in a home that had no real structure. Mine did. Several more inconsistencies were surfacing, like there was no religion; the family make-up was different. She had only two brothers, no sisters; I had five brothers and a sister. How was it connected with who she is and who I am?

Still, despite the differences, I was drawn to the book—perhaps because it was a way for me to prove Gary wrong, or maybe because her behaviors were similar to mine, or maybe it was simple curiosity. Then again, to my surprise, it was easy to understand reading. I finished all 219 pages of the book and decided there was nothing of a factual basis for Gary's ridiculous mention of this autism.

It was now Tuesday afternoon, and Mike was home from school very excited about some information on ditto sheets he had obtained off the Internet at school pertaining to autism. The information on these sheets were about behaviors the professionals look for with children who have the disability of autism.

I thought, "Good. Finally, a chance to show Gary was wrong, the bigmouthed bubblehead."

When Gary arrived home and his chores were completed, he reviewed the papers and laughed hard, stating, "Here we go. 'Difficulty mixing with others. Insists on sameness. Laughs inappropriately. Little to no eye contact. Insensitivity to pain.'"

I stood up and said in a strong voice, "Stop! That's enough, Gary."

He started laughing so hard and said, "Well, I'm sorry, but it's true!"

I said, "Oh yeah. Well, we'll just see about that. I'm going to ask my dad." Then I stuck my tongue out at him.

It was some time later before I talked to my dad about this. I guess it was due to my not knowing where or what to begin with. However, it was on a Saturday when I decided to call him as it felt right to do so, and also because I now knew how to arrange the order of my questions without leading him into answering them with statements he thought I wanted to hear.

I started with a simple question. "Daddy, I was wondering about something," and I started giggling. "Did I as a child have any unusual behaviors?"

Dad's response sounded puzzling to me. He said, "What?"

I continued by asking, "I mean, when I was little, did I have difficulties mixing with other children?"

His answer was "You had difficulty mixing with everyone."

I said, "Oh."

I giggled a little and asked the next question from the list Mike had given me. "Did I like change?"

He laughed and then stated, "No, you never could stand change."

Then the next, and the next. Each question was followed by answers confirming what Gary had said. Then I had one final question, which was to be the most painful of all. "Daddy," I asked, "do I have common sense?"

Well, he didn't answer in words. Instead, he laughed. It was clear to me that something was wrong with me, but I couldn't make any understanding that it was this autism.

I told Daddy the reason for the questions was that Mike had brought home papers about a learning disability. However, I did not tell him what it was. Daddy stated that I always had problems, particularly with communicating, and that I was not to use this as a crutch. His exact words were "Don't use it as a crutch."

I thanked him for helping me, told him I loved him, and hung up.

I sat down and started to cry. The words Daddy had spoken played over and over in my head. Memories of words my mother spoke when I was a child played over and over in my mind: "Don't talk to Susan; she wouldn't understand!" "Susan gets upset about everything!" "Damn it, what in the hell is wrong with that girl? She repeats everything you say." "Nobody understands what in hell you are talking about!" "Susan is so damn clumsy!" "Susan has no common sense!" "Susan doesn't have a sense of pain." "Susan, your thinking is all backwards." "Susan, stop your damn laughing; there's nothing funny about that!" "Susan fights with everybody!"

With the statements from my past spoken by my mother came more massive tears. However, the complete understanding as to the possibility of having autism was not registering any sense to me. More evidence of facts needed to be presented before me, and my constant insistence of the word *no* forced its way to my voice.

Then two weeks had passed, and the echoing words of broken pieces of information drove me to another source to find answers. I went to my grandfather's house with the paper of traits associated with the learning disability, in a new desperate attempt to seek the truth.

Grandpa listened closely to my copycat version of the conversation I had had with my dad. Then to my dismay, he spoke the exact words dad had said, and I laughed in the same manner as before. I told Grandpa I had accidentally stumbled on this information, and I was not in any way finding fault with the family, but I needed to know who and what I was about.

Grandpa gently smiled and told me again the same thing my father had, except he added that no one ever seemed to completely understand what I was talking about; and certainly, I was not able to understand what others were saying to me. He said I was always out of tune with conversation, reading more into what others were saying, and not responding correctly with my emotions.

I laughed harder, stating, "No, I just don't see why people can't speak proper English, and say what they mean, and mean what they say."

Grandpa smiled again then said, "Well, it's just one of those things. Don't let what others say bother you. You do alright!"

I smiled, then asked him, "If I am alright, then why? Why did the family pick on me so bad?"

He said, "Susan, it's because you were loud."

I laughed again, saying, "If it was just about being loud, then why would everyone correct the way I behaved?"

Grandpa said, "Well, Susan, some of your behaviors were different than the other kids."

I asked, "Like what?"

Grandpa sighed for a minute and then said, "Susan, I really don't think it's necessary to bring up your past, especially since you have blossomed so much since being with Gary."

I begged Grandpa to tell me.

He finally began to explain that I was very shy and quiet until someone would talk to me. When they did, I always seemed to be lost for an understanding. He went on to explain that people would try to help me by rephrasing their words, or by showing me with props; even then, I would become very upset, scream, or repeat over and over words or phrases. He said sometimes I would talk too fast, too loud, or not at all.

I stopped Grandpa for a moment to say, "Well, people would scare me!"

Grandpa continued by saying, "That's another thing. If people looked at you, you would panic with fear, cry, or get mad. You also would put your head against something and bang. One time, you were so out of control, your dad picked you up and put your head under cold water in the bathtub."

I told Grandpa, "I remember that, but no one was making sense. Of course, I was mad."

Grandpa looked at me and smiled, saying, "Your grandma always used to say, 'All Susan ever needed was more time to comprehend things.'"

I smiled back and said, "Grandma was right. She always could explain things so I could understand." I told Grandpa how I was always being corrected by Mom for things—you know, always being slapped. I said, "Mom would always be telling me to put my shoulders down, take my fingers out of my mouth, and lift my chin. I don't understand why she kept doing that." And I said, "Daddy used to say be myself, and when I was, I got in trouble. Daddy used to say I was a carbon copy of my mother, and she didn't like it."

Grandpa said, "Susan, your mother was not nice to you. Your dad, well, he meant well; but remember, it was very hard to talk to you when you were younger, especially when you were very young."

As I continued my conversation with Grandpa, my thoughts were repeating the word *autism*. I remembered hearing this for the first time when I was sixteen. I kept replaying the video of my stay in the hospital so many years ago.

I was finding it difficult to stay in touch with the on-going visit with Grandpa. As he went further into the discussion about my mother not being nice to me, he insisted that it was he and Grandma who found an appropriate place for me to reside so many years ago. He stated, "I told that doctor, 'My granddaughter does belong in the psychiatric center. She's not crazy! I don't want her on the street; she'll get killed. All Susan needs is time and proper guidance to process things.'"

Grandpa continued to go on with many stories of blame directed toward my mom. The scrambling of information became more and more intense inside my head. I told Grandpa I was ready to leave to go home since I now realized several hours had passed, and it was getting close to lunch. Grandpa hugged me and said, "Your grandpa loves you. Don't you forget that."

I said, "I won't. Thank you."

Now outside, I began the three-mile walk home. Most of the streets had been plowed from the many inches of snow, which had closed all the area schools. The air had warmed a bit. I think it was up to twenty-two degrees from the overnight low of five.

The weather was of no problem for me. The snow was a visual beauty. What was a problem was sorting all the information. "Could it be true?"

I was replaying the memory of my stay in the hospital. Doctor Murray Pulski, a respected area psychiatrist, told my parents at one of the family meetings, "Susan doesn't know who she is." He said, "When I first started working with her, I thought she might be schizophrenic because sometimes when I talked to her she sounds like a four-year-old; and other times, she sounds like a twenty-four-year old." He went on to say that, "As I researched schizophrenia, I concluded she does not have this disorder. Susan does not fit the profile."

During this family visit, I remember Mom and Dad breathing out of their mouths. I did not know why. I also did not know why Mom had such a hard time understanding me.

Dr. Pulski went on to say, "Susan does, however, fit the profile for autism."

My mom asked the doctor what that was. The doctor said, "It is a processing and communication disorder, which would require lifelong care."

Mom insisted, "My daughter does not have any problem communicating!"

The doctor continued to state, "Based on what I and the medical staff here have observed, along with what you and Mr. Bennett have shared with me about Susan's history, it is clear she has learned to connect words but lacks emotional understanding beyond a four-year-old."

Dad stated, "My daughter just doesn't want to grow up. She doesn't like change." Mom added, "Susan is just stubborn!"

Doctor Pulski commented further, "This is all part of the autism disorder."

I remember the conversation becoming more and more upsetting to me as the family meeting continued. I was also now repeating over and over the conversation with Grandpa. I could not put this together to make sense. Mom said I didn't have any problem communicating. Grandpa said I talked too fast, too loud or not at all. Then repeating words from the previous conversation with my dad—that I never liked change, that I had difficulty mixing with everyone, and that I had temper tantrums—no one seemed to understand that I had no sense of danger or of pain, that I did not make eye contact, that my thinking was backwards, that I had no common sense (actually Dad had laughed at that question). Still, all the words and phrases were just that: words and phrases with no meaning. I was not processing this with any useful content. I needed more proof.

I was now passing the church (Southside Baptist) that we attended on Sundays, when I replayed visual memories of the people who attended: Carol and

Bob, Jack and Teresa, George and Vonda, Duke and Vera, Lucille and Manny, Guy and Franny—Guy and Franny? They were the next people to call to find out about my childhood. These folks lived next door to my parents for many years. They knew Mom and Dad. They knew me when I was born till I was at least six years old. That was the answer.

I decided to call Franny on Saturday. I had a couple of days before to prepare proper questions without allowing myself to become upset from all the scrambling.

When Saturday arrived, I remember reaching for the phone several times, only to set it back on the cradle. What if she doesn't want to talk to me? What if she does and tells me the same thing Dad and Grandpa said?

I decided it was too important to me not to call. I dialed the number. Fran (as she preferred to be called) picked up the phone. I told her who I was. She was happy to hear from me. She wanted to discuss my current family matters and church issues. I was only interested in finding out information about my childhood.

This entire conversation with Fran was hard to balance. Fran did say that I did not talk until I was three or four years old. She said when I finally did start talking, I talked so fast no one could understand me. She went on to say that I talked so much, she swore I talked in my sleep. "Always talking and babbling on about some nonsense." She stated, "Susan, you seemed somewhat delayed in learning. I don't think you learned how to walk until you were three and a half or four." "You would scream a lot and carry on with temper tantrums when anyone tried to teach you new things." Fran went on to tell me of the potty-training story. She said, "Your mother would get mad at you because you knew what she wanted, you just didn't want to give it to her." Fran stated, "I have a lot of respect for your mother." She told me when I was expecting my son, "Never let anyone tell you how to raise your kids." Fran further added, "I never did."

The conversation with Fran went on for a while longer, and I began to understand that Mom did the best she could. I did not know just how much of a problem I was until after hearing many stories from people who struggled to work with my very intense behaviors. Soon, Fran told me that Guy (her husband) needed her assistance, and she could not talk with me anymore at this time. I told her, "Thank you," and that she was a big help.

I began to cry after I hung up the phone. I did not know why, but floods of tears came down my cheeks. I went to my room, sat on my bed with my blankie, and began to rock until I fell over on my side and fell asleep.

Several weeks had passed by since this phone visit with Franny, but the words and phrasing were not enough to prove any fact of this autism. Even matching up the words from the papers Mike brought home to the words that were spoken by family and friends did not give me any true understanding of the processing and communicating disorder labeled *autistic*.

I continued to speak with Gary about answering the repeating stream of questions related to this. Gary's thoughts at this time were to contact an area psychologist and see if a second evaluation was possible.

Several days had passed along with research through the phonebook for possibilities. Doctor Jeffrey Donner stood out to my husband; I do not know why. Gary made the call to his office only to discover from the secretary that the doctor was not in at this time. A short while later, a second call was made. Gary was connected directly to the man. As he spoke to him, Gary told many facts to the doctor about my communicating issues, behaviors, and emotional distress over the whole autistic matter. The conversation went on for about twenty minutes.

Gary told me that the doctor was certain that autism existed, but to test a person with such a high level of skills was impossible to do. The doctor said with Susan working a job and driving a car, it was not necessary to take his money to perform any kind of testing. He further added that if I were to have problems with my skills, counseling was certainly an option.

Even after the call to Dr. Donner, it was not convincing enough to prove this autism idea. After all, how can a person conclude a diagnosis simply from a phone call? What is this anyway? So I don't like changes. So I have temper tantrums. So I don't mix well with other people. So I laugh inappropriately. So I'm insensitive to pain (mostly) or I have no fear of danger. So I don't make eye contact (mostly). So I'm overactive. So I like simple, repetitive things. So I can have a good time by myself. So I have a good memory. No! I'm not deaf! I simply do not always want to respond to conversation. So lots of people do not like these things. So! So! So WHAT? Gee whiz, I want people to understand me. I'm not autistic.

What I did know was the morning routine and the evening routine gave me what I needed—structure. I liked doing the same things over and over and over. I did not like conversations with people. It seemed as if I was the observer and tape recorder. I always had to sort or organize the information. Following rules was easy; it gave me direction. Sometimes, though, it was hard to know what the rules were—especially since most people's topics of conversation were different than mine. The scrambling of words repeating in my ear are certainly not something I liked to do over and over, unless perhaps it was in the form of music. Whether it was a cartoon jingle, a commercial, or a fun song, everything else in word form had no sense or rhythm. It made little or no understanding for me. Without order or direction or rhythm, how could anyone possibly have fun in conversation? Autistic? No way—this was a sour note.

CHAPTER 9

FIRST DATING EXPERIENCE

Chapter 9 describes Susie's first dating experience and how she went from a shy, young, innocent-looking girl to a very mature and beautiful young lady by simply having her hairstyle and clothing changed. While in a group home, two of the adults thought it would be nice to give Susie a new look. So they changed her hairstyle, put on makeup, and gave her tight jeans, a knit stretch shirt, along with flat shoes, to boot.

This not only changed Susie's appearance, but it also changed her personality. She was very unhappy with this new look. She hated it. She hated the fact she no longer looked like Susie, while everyone else loved her new look. They thought she looked beautiful, like a model. Her new look led to a young man asking her to the movies. While at the movies, he touched her hand, which led her to becoming hysterical. She was very frightened by his touch and screamed out and ran out of the theater screaming.

Susie recalled this experience because of an incident that occurred with her son. He invited a young lady over to their home to visit, and the young lady was dressed in a low cut lacy blouse, and it brought back these memories. Unfortunately, because Susie did not understand the true meaning of dating, she tried to set ground rules for her son and this young lady; and they were both very offended, which caused a fight between Susie and her son.

This chapter also describes how Susie purchased a harp and fell in love with the feel and the sound of the harp. She had never played before but knew that she wanted one. It felt right for her to have it, and even though her husband thought she was wasting money, she purchased it and a book of children's music to go with it. It didn't take any time at all for Susie to realize that she was blessed with a natural gift for playing the harp. More and more, the music became part of her life. She played every day, and remembering the songs was very easy for her. It was very soothing and relaxing for her, and she was so proud of her accomplishment at learning to play the harp.

CHAPTER 9

My son was also hard to follow or understand. He almost always was angry or sad. Maybe he was autistic, and Gary got us mixed up.

Mike liked socializing. He liked his friends—Amy and Nicole, mostly. He was always talking on the phone or going to their homes for a visit.

One Saturday afternoon, Amy and Mike came to our home to—as he says—hang out. I insisted that his bedroom door remain wide open, a rule I requested from an early age when a friend came to visit. Mike was insisting the door did not have to be wide open. The more he pushed to have it closed, the more I pushed to have it open. He began to yell at me, saying I was not right. "Mom, you're autistic." "Mom, you're crazy." I told him if he did not stop the nonsense, his friend would have to leave.

A short while later I began to think about this teenager-dating thing. Although I did not date as a teenager, many kids did. I thought Mike and Amy had been spending a lot of time together in the last two months. I decided I needed to tell Amy where my rules are on the subject of dating. I asked Mike if he would go outside for a couple of minutes so I could speak with her. He did agree.

Once alone with Amy, we sat on the couch. I asked, "Are you in love with my son?"

She answered, "Oh yes, I think Mike is soooo nice."

I looked at the floor for a couple of seconds, then at the clock (it was 2:09 PM). I told her, "I'm sure he loves you too."

She giggled.

I now was looking at her mouth and said, "I want you to know I like you. I want you to know that you are always welcome to come to our home and visit, maybe even come for dinner."

She smiled bigger.

I looked down at her blouse, which was black, low cut, and lacy. I said in a stern voice, "I do not believe in fourteen-year-old children dating. I do not want this serious relationship to go on any further."

Amy stood up, went to the front door, opened it, and slammed it behind her. Mike came in almost seconds later, yelling, "What the hell did you say to her, Mom?"

I answered, "I simply told her you are too young to date."

He snapped at me, "I hate you!" Then he went outside.

I could not understand what I said wrong. I was just giving rules of direction for the children to follow. Well, I did not want any unnecessary stress to come into my head or house; but when I spoke words to others, they just insisted I needed to change my ways.

I did remember a dating arrangement made by the staff in the group home I once lived in. I was nineteen years old, and the treatment team of the house wanted me to socialize more.

The staff of the house consisted of Frank, Alan, Amy, and Bob. Frank and Amy decided I needed a complete makeover. This included my hair, clothes, and makeup. Their thoughts were, at the time, "Susie dresses the same all the time: like a school girl at a church picnic, prim and proper—boring!"

The staff never asked me why. Nor did they ask me what I wanted. The only thing I knew back then was family was not involved, and my behaviors were always a constant problem for others. People could not understand why I liked the same things, why I liked to have a routine or talk about the same subjects over and over.

Now these members of the staff were about to change everything I was. I could not have behaviors or the psychiatric center would be where they would send me—a place Grandpa said I did not belong. I'm not crazy.

The memory of this transition got clearer during those forty minutes Mike had been outside with Amy. I remember my hair being colored bleach blonde and my clothes being updated, from dress slacks and buttoned-up shirt with a ribbon around the collar, to Jordache jeans, a tight stretch knit top, heel boots, and makeup.

When Frank and Amy finished around my eyes, they smiled and stated, "Wow, Susie looks like a model!" They both were excited about the change. They turned me around toward the mirror.

I looked at myself a few seconds, then I cried. I cried and screamed. Frank and Amy were loud, stating, "What's the matter?" I screamed louder. Amy's voice was fast and high-pitched, saying, "Don't you like it?" Frank came over and put his hands on my shoulders.

I jerked into a stiff position, still crying. He insisted I was pretty before I started crying and got mascara running down my cheeks. His exact words were "This is ugly! The mascara is running down your face. Now get a tissue and wipe your eyes. Stop the nonsense."

I was afraid of all the changes and words. I was beginning to understand that much spoken phrase, "You cannot control the words or actions of others. You can only control how you react." These words were first introduced by my dad, then later repeated in different therapy sessions.

After a week had passed with this new look (I *hated*), a young man from the day program (of the psychiatric center) asked the staff from the group home if he could escort me to the picture show the entire house was going to see. The staff agreed, and Jim (the young man), along with Frank and Amy and the rest of the residents, walked down the street to the Elmira 1-2-3 Theater.

The movie was called *Body Heat*, a rated-R movie about a sexual relationship. I wanted cartoons or simple comedy. I did not like grown-up movies.

Jim and I sat next to each other in the row of seats directly behind the staff and residents. As I watched the screen showing lots of skin of the actor and actresses, I was puzzled by the story.

Then I felt a touch on my hand, and I jumped to a standing position and began crying and screaming. Everyone in the theater was looking at me. I shook with fear and continued to scream out, "He touched me! He touched me!" Frank and Amy came to the aisle I was standing in to talk to me, but I ran into the lobby screaming over and over, "He touched me! He touched me!"

I ran outside the theatre, sat down on the sidewalk, rocking back and forth, saying, "He touched me. He touched me."

Amy came over to me and kept saying, "Suz, it's alright. I'll take you home."

As we walked back, she asked me what had happened. I told her, "Jim tried to hold my hand." Amy started to laugh. I started to cry again.

Once home, the entire staff repeated for weeks to tell me this was all a normal part of the dating game.

My memory from twenty years ago was interrupted by the front door being forced open, then slammed. It was Mike growling at me as he raced through the house to his bedroom, then slammed that door.

I stood up from the couch where Amy and I had sat. I looked at the clock. It was 2:50 PM. I knew Gary would be coming home anytime, and soon, the evening routine would begin.

Gary did arrive within minutes. I talked to him about the afternoon. He told me I was wrong to have said anything.

I knew I was not happy about the whole subject; but I was happy about setting the table for supper, letting the dogs in the house for their supper, closing the blinds to the windows, picking up around the house, and all the rest of the evening chores. I do so like routine. I don't like conversations that do not make sense.

Monday morning arrived; and I was happy because this, too, was a routine that made sense. The drive to work with good ole Charley Pride seemed to put the rhythm back into my senses from the off-key rhythm of the weekend. Yes, order and structure were now in a visual form as I drove into the bus garage. David's van was in its proper place. Sherry's car and all the buses. Alta was in the hallway; so was Mr. Ike. In the office were Donna, Karen, and Ella. The day was organized, just as it should be, with all the people, things, and events. The days had passed into weeks, and weeks turned into months; and during this time, I had become more and more insistent to have order, and a true part of me was beginning to come to the surface.

Also, Gary and I were going to receive a good-size income tax refund, which we were to split in half. Each one could do what they wanted with the money.

I went to Knapps Music Store, where they sold musical instruments. I asked Dave, the salesman, if he had any harps. He told me the store had never sold any. He did look in the music catalog to see if he could order one.

Dave found a couple of harps, stating the prices: ten to twenty thousand dollars for a full-size harp. I did not have that amount of money. He went on to say that there was a smaller harp called the Irish or pixie harp. I looked at the picture and decided to have him order it. The price was right: $385, and I had four hundred dollars.

I went home and told Gary about my investment. He was mad. He said, "You don't even know how to play any instrument. Jesus Christ, whatever possessed you to buy it."

I said, "It feels right."

Gary got even louder, yelling out, "Honey, you don't spend that kind of money for something that feels right. You are a half-wit!"

I yelled back, "I am not!"

He further added, "You don't know how to read music, and I'm not paying for lessons."

I snapped at him, saying, "No one asked you to!"

Gary went on to say, "What in the hell do you want a harp for?"

I only responded by quietly saying, "I don't know."

He kept going on about how stupid my decision was. I only knew it felt so right inside me to have one.

About a week and a half later, Dave, from the music store, called to say that my harp came in. I went to the store right after work to get it. Dave had already put the strings on it. He explained that the red strings were C and the purple strings were F. He also said he himself had never played one before, even though he taught lessons to people on many different kinds of instruments (guitar, keyboard, piano, banjo).

Dave asked me if I wanted to purchase a book of songs. I told him, "I do not know how to read music, and my husband is not going to pay for lessons." Dave was silent for a minute and then suggested a number of books in which letters were placed on every note of every song in the book. I did not like those grown-up books—most of the songs I did not know. He asked me if I wanted children's music. I smiled so big and said, "Yes!"

He showed me a thick book called "The Big Book of Children's Songs." Yes, this was what I wanted. I paid him the money then took my beautiful harp home. Gary shook his head back and forth, saying that I was not going to learn how to play it, and that all that money was wasted. Mike was kind of supportive about my purchase. He said, "It's pretty, Mom, but it looks hard to play."

After supper and the evening routine, I took my harp and book on the couch. I plucked a few stings then picked up the book. Flipping through the pages, I found the song, Brahms's Lullaby. I again picked up the harp, followed along with the information Dave had given to me about the colors on the strings. Soon the sound on the strings emerged into music. I had learned my first song. It was slow but recognizable.

I remembered the song from a stuffed toy I once had in my crib as a child. Even though I screamed when the toy no longer played music because I did not know how to make it work, I now was playing the tune again on this instrument. I was so happy. I repeated it again and again and again. Perhaps I was slow, but so was the song. Yes, this is a very good thing.

The next day, I played Brahms's Lullaby over and over, along with a couple of new tunes: "Michael, Row the Boat Ashore," "Twinkle, Twinkle, Little Star," "Three Blind Mice," "The Farmer in the Dell." Within fifteen days, I learned fifteen songs. It was easy and effortless. I had found something that came to me naturally.

I did struggle with my elbows becoming tired from being in a horizontal position while playing. However, this was corrected when, by chance, an old "I Love Lucy" rerun appeared on television; and the guest star was Harpo Marx, a harpist from a comedy trio, The Marx Brothers. I quickly turned my instrument around and was no longer playing with tired arms. This made sense in two ways because now the sound box faced the audience, and my elbows were hanging down my sides—naturally.

A few days later, I comfortably added another thirty-five songs, bringing the total number of songs to fifty. Gary and Mike were amazed at my progress. I so much wanted to return to the music store to ask Dave what he thought.

A few days later, I was at the store, shaking at first; but I soon settled down into the rhythm of sound.

David said, "You never played before?"

I said, "No."

He said, "Don't go anywhere, I'll be right back."

He returned within a minute, bringing with him the owner of the store—John. Dave said, "Susie, play another song." I did. Dave and John both stood there with a funny look on their faces. I said, "What's wrong? Didn't I play it right?"

John said, "Young lady, you play like a fish to water."

I remember being puzzled by this because I was playing a harp, not being a fish swimming in water. Dave said, "Play another song." I did, and another and another. The two went on to talk about how they had never seen anything like it before. I only knew their conversation was becoming painfully difficult to understand or to follow. I thanked them for their time and went home.

More and more, my music became a part of me. I played every day. Remembering songs was easy. Remembering simple directions was easy. Understanding the words of others remained hard. I still could not get the intentions of others or ideas of others organized and sorted with any real rhythm. As time continued to pass, I found another way to relieve some of this stress. I found an old yo-yo in my toy box and decided it was a necessary tool to take with me to the bus garage, especially since my harp was not an option.

CHAPTER 10

PHYSICAL WAYS TO DEAL WITH AUTISM

Chapter 10 describes how stress affects Susie's life and how routine enables her to stay calm and focused. Susie has many ways to release stress, such as through the use of a simple toy such as a yo-yo, to walking on a curb and trying to maintain her balance while, at the same time, trying to regain balance in her life.

Susie needs to have a very external visual release when she is trying to regain her composure and make sense out of life. Most of Susie's life, she has been forced to deal with change based on what someone else has either said to her or told her to do. She has never been able to just do something for herself, on her own. She has always been told what to do. Her decisions have never been her own. She always focused on actions, not on words, to gain some sense of composure. But to give her security, it always came from the same source: her blankie.

CHAPTER 10

Even though I enjoyed the routine at work, the words from home played over and over in my head. I would try not to let my co-workers know just how stressed I really was, how on some days, behaviors could surface at anytime.

My yo-yo was a visual way to express the ongoing conflict in my thoughts. Yes, this toy gave a great release of stress to me. It was also well received by my co-workers. Up and down, up and down, first my left hand, then my right hand, up and down. As I began to improve with the yo-yo in my hand, harmonious arm-circling motions came without forcing any effort. Up and down, round and round, over and over, up and down, round and round, over and over. The procedure or action of the yo-yo gave the internal conflicts in my thoughts a very external visual release. The thoughts played over and over, the yo-yo motion went up and down, round and round, over and over. The harmonious circle motions came naturally. This was a change I was not aware of until the repetitive action took place.

Most of the changes in my life (up to this time) had been a forced effort by someone or some situation—not a natural quiet rhythm, but instead, a noisy scrambling of words or actions in which my world could no longer exist, except deep inside me. Doing what I was told gave a direction. Following rules gave a balance, especially when my emotions began to surface with intense force. I needed another visual action to help my emotions that had no quiet rhythm intact. Parking lot lines, tile floor seams, curbs, sidewalks, or road edges provided this. Walking a straight line—any straight line—gave direction in a visual form.

When stepping on curbs, seams, or parking lot lines, an awareness of balance became more important. I did not like uneven or broken lines as this was another reminder of what was not secure in my life. Balance—I NEEDED BALANCE. I walked on the lines while spinning my yo-yo. Up and down, round and round, over and over, straight and narrow.

Focusing only on the actions, not the words. The stress was becoming fuzzy, the relief was becoming clear. I had found harmony at work. I found harmony at home on my harp.

As time went by, the changes in my life that I had no control over seemed to be all around me. With my music, my blanket, the yo-yo, and routine, I had some control. The evening routine at home helped to drown out the irritating sounds from the television, telephone, my husband talking, my son talking, the bird squawking, the dogs barking, and any other noise overloading my senses.

The focus is on the task, not the nonsense. At the end of the day, my blankie wrapped me with more security. This made sense. The changes in the world around me included Sandra returning to the bus as a regular student, my first year at the garage coming to a closure, tenants in Gary's apartments moving in and out, working on the property where our house would be built, Mike going to high school, new faces at the garage, along with an old face—Garth.

CHAPTER 11

SCATTERED THOUGHTS

Chapter 11 finds Susie and her thoughts in life scattered all over the place. At the beginning of the chapter, she is focused on the coming of autumn and stresses in her life being reborn. In this chapter, she is trying to understand her son, Mike, and why his personality, behavior, and appearance have changed so drastically. She turns to her co-workers at the bus garage for answers but finds herself still confused as to how such an innocent, proper clean boy who once listened to easy listening music and church music could become a boy who wears baggy clothes and listens to loud heavy metal music.

The stresses become more and more difficult for Susie to handle throughout the chapter, which forces her to turn to something that will help her relieve the daily stress and to live life for her. She does this by purchasing a package of silly putty, which she is able to place in the palm of her hand when needed, and which allows her to release the built-up level of stress that is throughout her body.

In this chapter, Mike was also placed in a psychiatric center out of the area, which forced Susie to muster up all the courage she had, to drive miles and miles away to see her son. By the end of this chapter, Susie has accomplished one more thing in her life: the courage to travel out of her comfort zone to extend her love to her son.

CHAPTER 11

With autumn quickly arriving, a new series of problems and stresses surfaced. Processing such issues was slow; the events were fast. I relied on David to help me understand rules and boundaries in social situations or family matters. Ella helped me with conflicts. She was like having a gentle mom and teacher guiding me through everyday issues, some of which were raising a teenager.

My son was just starting high school, but he wanted the latest clothes, the newest music, and the coolest friends. I did not like this transformation at all. For me, awareness was necessary, so I did not have behaviors. My harp, yo-yo, blankie and routine provided some of this; still more was necessary.

Gary was of some help. He related many stories of his teenage years to me; still, part of his experiences frightened me more. Thus, new conflicts developed in my already overloaded memory circuits.

What I saw in Mike was not what he gave me in a visual or audio form. His attitude was negative—swearing, yelling, or lying. His clothes were dark colors and not formfitting (the baggy sloppy look). His music at one time was soft and smooth (classical, country, children's, spiritual, or uplifting). It was now rigged, choppy, and loud—rap, Marilyn Manson, Lenny Kravitz, to name a few. His room, which once had order, became a mess on an daily basis, like a tornado—clothes, books, papers, pencils and pens, and other items on the floor. The bed was unmade, the lamp shade tipped over, the curtains and blinds uneven. The pictures on the wall were uneven. Food, food wrappers, and soda bottles were scattered throughout the room; I did not allow food or drink in the bedrooms, not even mine. Incense and candles half burned were on the floor and the dresser; these items were not allowed to be in his room for safety reasons. CDs were out of their cases and scattered on the bed, dresser, floor, and desk. A glue gun of mine was buried under part of the mess. This, too, was not allowed for safety reasons.

I told Mike daily to pick up his room before his social time. Every day, he argued with me saying I was crazy. His eating habits were also inconsistent; he would pick at his food during dinner, stating he was not hungry, but came home from his friend's house complaining there was not anything to eat. Sometimes, he went into the kitchen and stuffed slices of bread in his mouth. Other times, he stuffed cookies, crackers, or chips into this mouth, as if he had not eaten in days. I noticed sores on his forearms. When I asked him about this, he stated, "A kid in school in art class accidentally burnt me with a glue gun." This made no sense to me because Mike was not enrolled in an art class at this time, and

I saw my glue gun in his room. I reminded Mike of this. His response was, "Mom, you are the one who has autism."

There was that word again, and I hated it. Words from my past repeated over and over. The conversation with my dad: "You never did like change," "You always had difficulty getting along with others." Then Dad's laughing when asked if I had any common sense. I had to know what this phrase meant.

The next day, while at the bus garage, my focus was on one question directed only towards co-workers: What is common sense?

I got many different answers along with plenty of laughter. I did not think this was funny, although no one knew. I asked all the folks, "Is a person born with this, or is this learned?"

Some laughed more, stating, "Anyone who doesn't have common sense has to be nuts." Some stated, "Well, I think it is a little of both." Still the answer to my question remained unclear; however, a direction was beginning to develop with the phrase, "I think it's a little of both." This puts the focus in the middle—a kind of balance—like walking on lines. It is a visual I can relate to.

Time and conflict continued between me and my son. Gary, however, was waiting to look at a Volkswagen Beetle he discovered in the newspaper want ads. He wanted me to have the type of car I liked from years ago. We did agree that it was a good investment. And so I was, at this time, the new owner of a 1973 Super Beetle customized show-quality Volkswagen. I did drive it only a few times to and from work before the colder weather set in; after all, the month of October was coming to an end. I was happy because it was another security of comfort for me: driving on roads for direction, laws to follow for direction, and something old to hold on to for security.

But shortly after this purchase, another series of events took place that shifted the security of direction off balance. This was Mike! At home, I knew there was conflict. The school was now at conflict with his behavior. Interim reports came, one or two at first, followed by phone calls from the office. He had been skipping school, having power struggles with teachers, and yes, temper tantrums. He threw a chair, knocked students' books on the floor, and did other physical acts causing concerns.

Mike did not seem to be sorry for his actions. Gary's thoughts were that Mike had no conscience. This word had some meaning for me.

The next day, at the bus garage, I asked the question to co-workers: "Are you born with a conscience, or is it learned?" Many of the co-workers I asked said, "It was learned." Some said, "You are born with it, but you must be taught how to develop and use it." I knew I had asked a variety of folks who had previously worked in different fields such as nursing homes, the prison, law enforcement, transportation, construction, factories, farms, ministries, child care, homemaking, newspapers, department stores, the psychiatric center, and special needs. I knew a conscience was knowing the difference between right and wrong. But if it was not clear, just keep following rules.

Mike did not want any part of this. He continued to argue with everyone about following any of the rules, especially me, insisting I was crazy.

I thought about my first year at the bus garage, remembering Gary pushing me to socialize, Sandra breaking her ankle, Garth leaving, autism, dating, and my harp. The focus now was on dating. The question was, "Were Mike's problems because I did not allow him to date?"

The next day I went to the bus garage. I asked many folks, "What is a good age to allow a teenager to date?" Again, many folks' answers varied. Some said fourteen years old, while others said sixteen years old. A few of the folks felt a sixteen-year-old teenager should have a parent close by to observe any inappropriate contact with the opposite sex. This made sense because more rules of order gave a direction.

Mike did not agree. He insisted I was wrong. The stress was becoming more and more intense on a daily basis.

My driver (Mr. Ike) and the children only saw a playful-but-guiding individual who cared about their well-being and the safety of all of them. Sometimes, after all of the children had departed from the bus, I found myself sliding down in the seat, biting down on my left index finger. I knew this would not be accepted if I continued. I had to find another way to release stress in a visual way. The yo-yo was not a practical tool to use on a school bus; walking on lines was not a practical choice, nor was my harp or music. What then could I do to relieve stress without having bad behaviors? The answer quickly came during a trip to the grocery store.

Gary had sent me to Tops to buy dog biscuits, bird food, candy, and a roasting chicken that was on sale—buy one, get one free. The chickens were at the end of the aisle where the holiday items were sold.

While passing through, I saw a product called Big Putty. This was an almost copycat version of Silly Putty. The colored plastic eggshell contained matching-color putty: pink shell, pink putty; orange shell, orange putty; green shell, green putty; yellow shell, yellow putty. Four colors to choose from. I only had twenty dollars in my pocket. The price was $2.99 each. Which color should I pick? This decision was hard because each color represented a different idea; for example, the color pink represented hearts (Valentines), girls clothes;

softness (my blanket is pink and white). The color orange represented pumpkins at Halloween (Halloween had scary things); orange is the color of some flowers or types of fruit. The color green represented natural visuals like trees, plants, and grass. The unnatural visual is money (although money is necessary for people's survival in today's living). The color yellow represented fruit (bananas, lemon—sour), smiley faces, and rays of sun light.

Light gave people direction. This made sense—another visual I was beginning to relate to. I remember as a child sitting on the bench swing of our swing set. This was also the summer that Sunbeam bread enclosed a free flat sunbeam whistle with every loaf of bread. My brothers were blowing the whistles in many different directions. This sound hurt my ears. I looked up at the sun, staring directly into it. The rays warmed my face while my eyes stayed focused on the natural direct connection.

I chose the yellow Big Putty to buy.

When I got home, I put the putty in the palms of my hands and rolled it over and over and over. This motion gave the internal replaying of words and actions of my son's recent behaviors a very external visual release. The biting down on my finger was now replaced with this soft round yellow putty toy—a more acceptable choice when others were not.

A few days later, Mike requested a composition notebook that he said was necessary for school. I gave him an extra one from the school supplies I had stocked up on months earlier. He quickly went to work on some writings. Some days passed, then an evening of verbal arguing and behaviors resulted in the police locating my son and taking him to the emergency room at St. Joe's Hospital.

The writing in the notebook explained why.

Mike had written many pages of being tired, sad, and the words "death seems to be the best option." I saw my son in the hospital observation room. He was nasty and demanding when he spoke to me. A nurse insisted he stop treating me with disrespect. Mike's response was "Mom doesn't care. She has autism."

This word was spoken again—*autism*. I began to cry.

Soon, it was time to go home as visiting hours were over. Once home, I told Gary of the events then picked up my harp. While I played "Silent Night," I cried and continued to cry through every Christmas song I knew at that time. Christmas was less than six weeks away. Still the internal scrambling played a very intense external sound. This made sense. Instead of screaming out loud, I let my fingers scream out rhythmical sound. Although the songs were about a baby named Jesus (the light of the world) and his mother, I related because I am a mother of a son, who brought light to me; and now the light was dying.

In the morning, I went to work and spoke to my boss, Alta, about the evening before. She gave me permission to take the rest of the day off to be with my son.

St. Joe's made arrangements for him to be admitted to a psychiatric facility in Buffalo, three hours away. Another arrangement made included plainclothes officers in an unmarked police car to transport him. I was to follow them in my vehicle.

I stayed close behind, keeping visual contact with the car, my speed, traffic, the signs, and the rules. This helped keep the conflicts of emotional scrambling away from the external surface.

Soon, we arrived. The routine procedures at Brylin were independent interviews with me, my son, and then both of us together. Mike told the staff, "My mom has autism and gets things mixed up." I did not like this word. We finished the admissions paper work, followed by instructions of necessary things to bring for the next trip up to see my son. I wanted Mike to smile, but he was angry.

Before I left, the staff gave me written instructions to guide me back home as the officer's part was no longer available. It was November 16, 2001, at 7:47 PM. I followed directions: "As you leave the exit off ramp, turn left onto Delaware Ave." This is a traffic circle. Also, there was construction and detours. The paper did not tell me what to do. It was dark outside, making visual direction difficult.

Soon, a gas station was in sight. After filling my tank, I asked the man, "How do I get onto Interstate 90 South?" He told me, "You just stay on the main road." I did, until more construction, more detours caused conflicts. I saw a sign with a route number going south. Even though it did not match the paper, I did know a sign going south was simple and clear to understand. All the visuals for driving, speed, rules, or traffic were clear. I kept a constant awareness of all signs going south.

Fragment images of Mike were entering my thoughts; words spoken replayed over in broken parts, and my senses were overloading. Tears came to the surface on and off. The internal was becoming an external, but all the visuals around me gave a direction to follow. The roads I traveled on were becoming farther from traffic, houses, and lights. Signs going south were more and more distant from one to the other. Still, this was my focus as I know I lived only seven or eight miles from the Pennsylvania border.

Soon, after hours passed, a sign appeared with a name of a town I remembered hearing before on an *I Love Lucy* rerun: Jamestown. I remembered, too, a segment on the *Today Show* of a map of the state of New York because Jamestown was the center of attention because of a discussion of Lucille Ball's hometown. The map showed this town being west of my town. Jamestown was the direction necessary to get home.

Once there, I looked for signs heading east. I saw one ahead with another name of a town I could relate to: Corning, New York, the Crystal City. They made glass; glass is clear.

As I drove, tears became more and more intense. What was not clear is Mike. I pulled over on the side of the road and put my four ways on so that cars from behind me would know I was there despite the darkness of the night.

I prayed for God's guidance to keep Mike safe. I also asked for wisdom, acceptance, and strength for all of us. This moment of silence was interrupted by a tractor trailer honking his horn as he went by. I dried my eyes with the backs of my hands and then continued home, focused on the rules of the road.

Finally, I was through Corning, Big Flats, and West Elmira, heading into my driveway. Once inside, I found Gary asleep in his chair. He woke up immediately with a stream of questions and statements: "Where have you been? Jesus Christ, honey, I thought something had happened to you. How come you're so late? It's almost one in the morning!"

After sharing my experience with Gary, I prayed once again and fell asleep.

The routine at work soon followed the next day, although my world inside my head was scrambling for understanding. I played over and over Mike's life, so far, remembering experiences of his childhood. Still, the main focus was on the children's safety and rules of conduct on the bus. Fragment images continued to break through my concentration of duties. The Silly Putty in my hand, when appropriate to have, I would squeeze in my palm. I would quickly roll it back into a ball, only to find myself repeating the motion. I needed another visual to help me.

I did speak to my boss, Alta, after the morning run—about the trip to Buffalo and what the staff wanted in regards to a weekly family meeting. The distance between the two locations, along with the work schedules, made the necessary meeting arrangements difficult. Alta decided that Wednesday afternoons would be honored for time off to make one of two weekly visits possible. The other day would be Sunday, along with daily phone calls to the hospital staff or Mike.

When I returned home later this morning, the empty house brought immediate tears. I wandered into my son's room. There was debris all over. Had I caused Mike's life to become such a mess? I began picking up the clothes, books, papers, CDs, candles, incense, and other items. The memories of my life with him were becoming clearer, along with the events from fifteen years earlier that brought his father and me together.

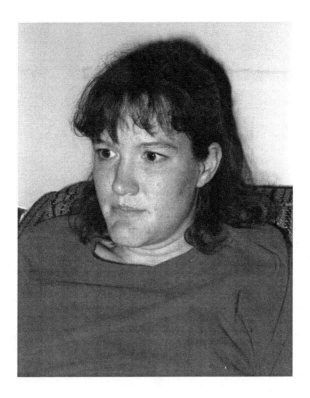

Chapter 12

MY MARRIAGE ENDS AS MY CHILD'S LIFE IS ABOUT TO BEGIN

Chapter 12 finds Susie rediscovering not only who she is but if she will be able to handle being a single mother, raising her baby on her own. At the beginning of this chapter, we see Susie going through many steps to become independent, by force, not because she is ready to. Once her good friend Jim passed away, a close family friend, Dennis, pushed himself into her life and married her within a matter of only a few months. Susie was not ready for this marriage emotionally or physically and, as a result, was emotionally and physically abused by Dennis. Only when she learned that she was pregnant and being beaten once more did she realize she had to walk away from this marriage in order to protect her baby's life.

CHAPTER 12

Long ago, at the age of twenty-three, I was on SSI disability for communication comprehension difficulties, depression, and anger issues, which always resulted in self-injury behaviors. The doctor had put me on a heavy dose of antidepressants, mood stabilizers, sleep aids, and other medicines for side effects. The psychiatric center day program also offered structure and direction for addressing these issues: group therapy, swimming (which I hated), psychodrama, individual therapy, social groups (cooking committee, cleanup committee, gardening committee), bowling, along with—but not limited to—weekly visits with the nurse for eating problems.

Ginger, the nurse, was concerned about weight loss—I was then 108 pounds. My speech was either too slow, too fast, or not at all. Eye contact was not present, tears came easily, and physical contact by others caused me to pull my body tight with fear. Rocking was not accepted, flapping my hands was not accepted, repeating words or statements from others was not accepted, screaming was not accepted, banging was not accepted, being alone and having my blankie was not accepted—a long list of don'ts was added. What was accepted was doing what I was told or more medicine would be added to the list of artificial means to correct any behaviors folks thought were odd.

Also during this time, Jim (the young man mentioned earlier in the story of dating) and I became good close friends (not lovers as touch was still an issue). We lived in the same apartment house. He lived out front in a room. I lived out back in a small apartment. We ate dinner together, fished together, walked to and from program together, along with Friday evening card playing with friends. All was routine until an explosion in my kitchen caused third-degree burns over 90 percent of Jim's body, resulting in his death.

Jim's lifelong friend since grade school, Dennis, was at the funeral services. Dennis did not appear to be sad about this, but I thought everyone deals with death in their own way. I was so devastated by this; still, behaviors could not surface.

Soon, I was under the guidance and direction of Dennis. He had always worked, never been on the system, no legal issues, clean in appearance, drove a car, no previous marriages or children. He came from a Catholic family, the same as I did. Although he made frequent visits during that past year to see Jim and me, Dennis and I were married within four months. My senses were overloaded, making processing difficult. I looked for security in routine, order, and direction.

A few months later, I found myself involved with yet another agency—the safe house, a hidden place where battered women and children go to be protected from others' abusive ways.

I did not understand many things about this either. The words *abuse*, *alcoholism*, *drug addiction* or *legal matters*—a few hours in this safe house created more conflicts in my head from these words that were spoken. The staff's emotions on the subject were also difficult to follow. The fears from within me were much too difficult to contain inside me, and I ran home to what I was familiar with.

By the time the fourth of July came, the words from the staff at the safe house were beginning to match up to Dennis' actions. During that evening, however, I remember getting a split lip, being kicked in the left kidney and lower back; and my blouse was ripped completely in the front. I yelled, but no one came. I wanted to go back to the psychiatric center, where it was safe. I now wanted out, or at least, I kept thinking about it.

But how? Lots of conflicts, no behaviors. My dad used to say, "Susan, you cannot run away from your problems." The Church said, "You don't divorce." The psychiatric center staff said, "No behaviors." The safe house staff said, "You cannot change an alcoholic or a drug addict."

My family did not understand me, the staff did not understand me, and now I did not understand me. Words with little to no meaning—I did not understand my own thoughts or, for that matter, even my body. Why did it have to be forced on me to have relations when I was so sensitive to touch? This whole thing was making me sick to my stomach and dizzy. I knew everything was out of sorts, including my monthly when I missed it.

I soon found myself walking through the drug store searching for the answer why. I am always on time for my period. I also knew that Dennis threw away my birth control pills in a fit of rage, along with all the other medicines months earlier. He pushed on me while saying very firmly, "My wife doesn't need pills! All she needs is me!" Still, I knew something was wrong. Little guidance was available as the day program was no longer a part of my routine. Dennis wanted nothing to do with the system. He said, "Too many people are telling you what to do!"

I walked over to the pharmacist and asked him what he would suggest. His response was funny: "Young lady, I think you better buy a home pregnancy test."

I said, "A what?"

The man repeated, "A home pregnancy test. They are right here on the shelf." He pointed over the counter to the shelf below.

I did as I was told, but I was scared again of yet another word: *pregnancy*. Once home, I kept the box out of sight for reasons that are still unclear today. The next morning, I quietly followed the directions on the box.

It was true. I was pregnant with Mike.

Standing in the bathroom with the positive result in my hand, I met a flood of questions I had no immediate answers to. In the next room was a man I no longer wanted to be with. What then was I to do? Words from others replayed over and over in my head, tears came, and so did sensitivity to sounds. I heard Dennis moving around in the bed. I knew I could not let him see me cry. Quickly, I dried my eyes with the hand towel; and then I hid the wand in the box, placing it between some folded towels on the shelf.

For a while, the day went on as usual, the routine of household duties followed by wife duties. As the time went by, the answer to one question became clear: Could I be a mother of a child? Yes!—with proper guidance and direction, especially because I was good at following orders, routine, rules, and remembering the good things taught to me by Mom, Dad, Grandma, Grandpa, staff, teachers, and friends.

Now I needed to tell Dennis the news. He was happy at first, then seemed to be distant from the whole idea after a few days had passed.

Another episode of rage surfaced one evening. He pushed me to the floor after a discussion about saving money for the insurance deductible needed for prenatal care. He kicked me in the left kidney and lower back again, stating he needed the money for something else. I knew now I had to get out; my baby was not safe.

Tears came heavy down my cheeks as I remembered those days long ago. Mike was not safe, yet now he kept making comments about me having autism. What was making him so sad and angry? He was so distant from me, but his things were right in front of me as I continued to pick up his room. The baby I wanted to keep safe from harm was older, among strangers in a strange place, with strange ideas. There was nothing I could do to stop it.

Was Mike afraid of me? Was he afraid that he has autism? Again, a heavy flood of questions with no answers and processing issues mounted daily, and another visual was necessary to release the conflicts.

CHAPTER 13

SUSIE LEARNS TO FACE THE REALITY OF BEING A SINGLE PARENT

Chapter 13 finds Susie's life in a state of upheaval. She learns that she is pregnant and yet finds herself being married to a man whom she doesn't love or trust. Her only ally is a friend of hers who helps her move out of her home and into a safe house, only to fall into the hands of the social services and a judge who convinces her she needs to go home and allow her unborn baby to be raised by both parents. She tries this for a little over a year until she is beaten so badly by her husband that not only does social services step in to help her but also the district attorney's office, when they find out the truth about her husband.

This chapter shows us not only what a strong woman Susie is but how she is also a woman who does what she is told to do even though she knows it is wrong. This chapter shows us how simple Susie really is. She is a woman who will do as she is told—one who follows directions even if her own safety is at stake.

CHAPTER 13

Once back at the garage for the afternoon run, I found a note in my mailbox. All drivers received one. I read the information then folded it neatly in half, to prepare for additional folding to place in my pocket.

Instead, I found myself folding the paper back and forth, making the crease weaker and weaker. I tore the paper neatly in half and then continued to fold the half pieces neatly, tighter, tearing each in the same way.

Smaller and smaller but uniformly, each part of the original paper began to take on yet another visual release. The whole paper represented a picture, such as a completed jigsaw puzzle—a visual photo composed of hundreds of little pieces. The ditto sheet in its total order represented a visual without a photo.

As I tore the paper into little identical pieces, each piece represented one part of words or phrases scrambling in my head. These paper pieces had not yet became a whole understanding with a picture image. Instead, I put each little piece of paper on top of each other in a neat order, wrapped with a rubber band. Perhaps when a visual understanding develops, I can throw all the pieces in the air (like confetti) to celebrate the true meaning of words.

In the process of arranging all the pieces in order, like a cube, thoughts became solid instead of scattered, thus some security was now present. More and more days passed along with additional thoughts scrambling. The paper folding provided order in a visual form. The yo-yo provided a visual release. The silly putty, walking on lines, and playing my harp all provided me with a necessary tool to keep my overloaded senses from becoming out of control. Self-abuse was no longer a damaging concern because the energy was being channeled in a positive way.

The staff at the hospital continued to gather information about Mike's history through daily phone calls. My memory played over and over like a video tape being rewound then played back. Again and again, images of Dennis and I came back clearer than the one before. Wanting out of that marriage was one thing, but getting there was another.

Even way back, my understanding of the world as it is and how I saw it were difficult to sort. It was two worlds, one mind. I took words literally. Others did not. Some people said I was naive. Still others said I was slow, socially clumsy, and odd. "People mean what they say, don't they?"

The time shortly after the news of my pregnancy and Dennis' episode of rage about money, I was prompted to call an old friend of Jim's and a regular patient at the day program.

This was Kevin. He, too, had issues in which medicine and therapy were necessary. Kevin also lived in the same apartment house as Jim and I. He was a daily visitor.

While Dennis was at work, I made a phone call to Kevin. We discussed many things, including the suspicious circumstances surrounding Jim's death, Dennis' odd behaviors, and the danger I was in. Kevin insisted that Dennis had something to do with the fire. He also insisted that I get out of there now. "Where would I go?" I asked. He told me he would drive from Corning with his truck to get me. He added, "Pack up everything you have. I will be there soon." I did as I was told.

Even then, processing words and statements from others caused scrambling. I was no longer on medicine, and I was carrying a baby. In the newspaper, the fire investigators listed the explosion as suspicious. I was not there in the apartment at that time, and Kevin also was not there. Why, then, would he say, "I know Dennis had something to do with the explosion?" Fears began to come to surface as I raced around the small apartment gathering all my things.

In less than an hour, Kevin showed up. My things were loaded onto the truck, and we were headed for Corning. I spent a few days with Kevin but did not like the idea of me sharing space with him.

Another phone call was made from his phone to the safe house. I kept the number from the first time I visited the house. Once again, I came to that place. The women helped me with guidance and family court, as well as protection.

The family court judge did not feel the same as all the others did about safety for me and my unborn child. He said, "You and your husband have not been married a year, and you have a baby on the way. It is the opinion of this court that through counseling, you both can work out your problems for the sake of your child." He also added, "Young lady, I suggest you follow through with additional therapy for your own problems." The court's decision had to be carried out as directed.

Dennis and I lived in separate apartments while we worked through our problems. Seven months later, we were living together, awaiting the arrival of our child.

The excitement of the baby kept our spirits up, and soon, Mike was born on Easter Sunday. The first fifteen months of Mike's life was a happy time for me. I learned how to read aloud to him from children's picture books. I had a routine. I made him laugh. I watched him learn, and I protected him from harmful things.

But all was coming to an abrupt end. Dennis' addiction issues and attitude were becoming worse. Sadly, only I knew—until another more violent episode of rage resulted in paralysis of my right leg (from being pushed into a corner part of a counter, injuring the lower part of my back), a split lip, a black eye, facial cuts, and a lump on my head (from being hit on the head by a cast iron grate from our stove). The police came only because I yelled to the tenant upstairs to call the police.

Thank god, she heard me. Thank god, it was July, and the windows were opened; and thank god, it took only one quick call for help before Dennis put his hand over my mouth, pushed my head into the refrigerator, and told me to shut up. Thank god that the police were involved.

My son's safety was all that I understood. Everything else was a scrambling of words and phrases in the hope of finding a direction in which to do this. The hospital staff, the safe house staff, the legal staff, welfare staff, SSI staff, and other agencies joined forces to keep my son and me from further harm. A visit to the district attorney's office to speak to Mr. Trice (my old friend) also helped.

It was there all the secrets Dennis ordered me to keep were now out in the open. Mr. Trice heard about the guns Dennis had, about shooting at me, about his drugs, about his friends (some of which, Mr. Trice had put in prison), about Jim's death, and all the stories of my history with this man. I also gave him photographs, lots of names (thirty-three in all) and addresses.

My friend Mr. Trice called an undercover detective from the Sheriff's Department to join us in the conference. It was during this time both men felt that Jim's death was a result of foul play in which Dennis was involved.

Placing Mike and I in hiding was necessary, but weeks turned to months as complications mounted. No proof, only circumstantial, followed by city court vs. family court issues. My physical injury and infant son, along with poor communication, played a part in the long process of achieving this goal.

At one point during my thirty days at the safe house, before I went back to our old apartment while preparations were still being worked out for our relocation, a staff told me very directly, "Do not let your emotions show, or your son will be taken away from you, do you understand? Do not cry or get mad. Let the system do its job."

I never forgot her words. I did not want my son taken from me. Finally, the relocation plans were in order. Mike and I had moved out of town. My divorce was also being processed, but all was not settled, I suppose because we were alone in a new place and no one but agencies knew why. I was not to discuss the matter with anyone else—more secrets for different reasons; more conflicts; no behaviors, no attitude, just doing what I was told to do.

Taking care of Mike was calming. Seeing him smile, teaching him manners, routine, and keeping him safe certainly made my days focused in a positive way. I liked teaching him numbers, names of objects, letters, and words. This was fun. I, too, learned so much.

Mike did not know how the sound of a loud muffler of a car sent fear inside of me, like the sound of Dennis' car. Instead he only knew I picked him up, held him close, and then walked along the sidewalk (I had not at this time mastered the art of driving, even though I was twenty-six). I may have had paralysis in my right leg and a prosthetic back brace, but keeping him in my arms was better than letting him go.

Mike did not know that a phone call with no voice at the other end sent waves of fear. All he knew was I picked him up and held him close.

CHAPTER 14

STARTING OVER

Chapter 14 finds Susie alone, starting over in a new city many miles from her family and friends. During this time, away from her family and friends, Susie had to become more independent than ever. She learned to survive through phone calls to the old safe house and visits to new local agencies in the area. She began to get back into the normal routine of visits to the therapist to help her get her life back on track. She was forced to deal with visits with her son and Dennis, which was a challenge to her. Only at night, when she was in her own bed, was she allowed to let her emotions loose and break down and cry herself to sleep. No one really knew of the trauma that Susie was going through as she had to conform to what society and those around her wanted, when inside she was literally falling apart and very scared.

CHAPTER 14

During the ten months of living away from my hometown, many new experiences, both good and bad, developed. I continued, however, with phone calls to the old safe house and the new one, as well as regular visits to new local agencies in the area.

One particular agency was a mental health clinic recommended by the new welfare program staff. I visited the clinic and discussed all the events that led up to my coming to the new town. After about an hour and a half, the intake person set up a therapist appointment schedule for the next week. Upon entering this office and beginning my discussion with this man, his response to me seemed less than comforting.

I said, "You don't believe me, do you?" The man said nothing. I took a paper out of my wallet from the district attorney's office and showed this to him. He read it then stated with a fast, rapid voice, "Don't go away."

The therapist left the room quickly then returned with another man. Then both men apologized for their behavior, stating, "Lady, you don't know how many people come in here with stories. We didn't know yours was true. Might we suggest Family Services as they are better certified at dealing with domestic abuse cases than we are?"

Again, I did as I was directed. Soon, I was settled in yet another therapy environment repeating my experiences, all the while remembering the rules of conduct taught by family, staff, legal, or teachers: no behaviors, no emotional outbursts of any kind.

Inside, the scrambling became more and more difficult to process, but my son kept any release of energy channeled positively.

Visitation between my son and Dennis was even more challenging. Dennis did get charged with third-degree assault after the police came, but he never did jail time. Instead, he claimed that I was unstable, crazy, and difficult to understand.

Family court was not sure how to handle all the information taken from all the parties involved, so visitation was honored; but safe house staff, the police, and child welfare kept a close eye on the situation. Mike and I took a bus from our new town to the old. A safe house staff met us at the bus station. Dennis met us across from the police station.

When a weekend visit was over, we met across from the police station; the safe house staff then escorted us into the police station. In there, the safe house staff evaluated Mike's attitude, physical condition, and belongings. When she determined that all was fine, we were escorted to the bus station to return to the new town. Many numerous precautions were in place to protect my son and me.

After every day passed, my 9:00 PM bedtime arrived; I, too, would lock all doors and windows, throw my blanket over my head, and rock back and forth, crying. This was the only time I was allowed to release any of my emotions. The blanket muffled the sound. I did not want Mike to be afraid.

As time went on, the news was delivered to me that my mom was dying of cancer. Although my family stayed distant from my issues, it was decided by them that I return to my hometown. I was expected to be available to care for Mom while Dad was working. Other family members had jobs and family duties or lived too far away to help.

CHAPTER 15

DISCOVERING YOUR SON IS GAY

Chapter 15 finds Susie struggling with a new reality in her life: her son being gay. This realization has Susie reaching out towards others to reassure her that being gay is a person's choice, and that it is possible for her son to change his sexual preference to be a woman.

However, the more people she questions, the more she hears that it is not a personal choice but that a person is born with this. It is as natural to that person as being the person you are. Susie is very angry and confused as to how this happened to her son. He was a normal little boy who faced much trauma throughout his childhood; and now, finding out that he is gay, she has to ask herself if she may be at fault.

During this chapter, Susie also had to deal with her son going into a psychiatric center, not once, but twice; and then instead of returning home, going to a foster home. This chapter forced Susie to confront many emotions such as confusion, sadness, anger, and fear of the unknown.

CHAPTER 15

After ten months of hiding, we returned to my old town with continuing guidance of all the agencies. Luckily for us, we later discovered that Dennis was following close behind at the new town. Whatever secret planning preparations were being made to move us out of the area, it seemed Dennis knew many details of those private talks.

Apparently, he had bought a baby room monitor identical to the one I used all the time for Mike. People who came to the old apartment (where Mike and I lived in before moving away to a different location) thought it was odd that Dennis would park his car at the carwash behind our house and sit there for long periods of time. He would call me immediately after someone left, after I got off the phone, or shortly after I returned home, demanding answers to his questions: "Why did you go to the district attorney's office?" "How come you told them I followed you?" "So where are you moving to?"

One visitor asked if I had the monitor on all the time. I said, "Yes." His thoughts suggested Dennis was listening through another walkie-talkie. So we disconnected the whole unit.

Dennis himself confirmed a few years later that was how he did it.

Many times, Dennis told people I was unreliable, crazy, or a social outcast due to communication problems. Worse, he continued even after I returned to my hometown, and years later, during the on-again, off-again visits with our son and the family court judge.

A short while after coming back to my hometown, settling into our new apartment, my divorce getting finalized, and mom passing, I developed a steady friendship with my landlord, Gary (later, he became my husband). He is twenty years older, an only child, and a very strong communicator. He owns his own business; has apartment houses; raises and shows Old English bulldogs; has been president of the local kennel club many times; was president, district president, state chairman, and awarded JCI senatorship of the Jaycees.

He was well liked by many residents and disliked by others. However, he was best known for telling it like it is.

Gary allowed me to paint my apartment, along with helping him clean out, mow, or paint others he rented. He could not believe I made it so far in my life because, he said, I used childlike wording and had a very regimented, simple, uncomplicated, and old-fashioned routine. He said I was shy, withdrawn, and uninterested in getting to know the world outside of my apartment, also adding that I see good in everyone.

Gary decided I needed him to help me understand life better so I could be a stronger person.

Whatever the reasons, he and I worked together on many things over the years, including caring, providing for, and directing Mike the best we could to prepare him for his adult life. I remember many good times and many times of friction in deciding a healthy path in which we wanted Mike to travel. Still, all efforts landed Mike in another psychiatric center called Brylin.

The other time was five years earlier, when Mike was nine years old. Mike was admitted to Benjamin Rush for a short stay, but visits with his father came to an abrupt end.

My son had many difficult challenges growing up, mostly with his father, but now he kept the focus on me: Mom has autism.

While at Brylin, Gary discussed with the doctor the possibility of Mike having autism due to his early childhood behaviors, his limited interest, and his difficulties getting along with others. The hospital clearly felt autism existed with me but was not certain it existed for Mike.

After six long weeks at the hospital, it was decided by all that he needed additional care. My son did not want to come home to live with me, nor did he want to be admitted to another psychiatric center. It had been decided that Pathways therapeutic foster care was the only other sensible place for him to be cared for.

Mike was scared of this idea. I, too, was afraid. Instead of prolonging his stay at Brylin while preparations were being made, Mike was allowed to come home. He was heavily medicated, home tutored, and had weekly therapy visits at Family Services.

We asked our neighbor Miss Beverly to look after Mike while I worked. Gary took Mike with him the other times, when she was not available.

Soon it was time for this huge transition of separation. Neither Mike nor I was completely settled by this, but he kept insisting that I could have done something to stop it. The good thing was he lived less than a quarter mile away. He could see his friends and come home on weekends. As a family, we attended weekly family counseling, daily phone visits, along with other activities the program offered; but again, all efforts failed.

Mike went up and down with behaviors and attitude. He continued to act out at school, gave the caregivers a hard time, and once was caught sneaking out of his bedroom window.

During those fifteen months Mike stayed at this home, the counselors and foster parents tried hard to determine why. We asked about getting another evaluation from a psychiatrist to decide if Asperger's syndrome might be the reason. This is another form of autism. The counselors made the arrangements. This was to be done by Dr. Donner, the same man who decided that autism existed with me.

Gary and I together visited with Dr. Donner. He made up his mind more quickly about his conclusions regarding me, maybe because, as he said, I talk a lot with my hands.

Again, Mike's history was necessary for testing. I provided Dr. Donner with copies of all my son's report cards. I told him of all the therapy agencies he was ever involved with, including at the age of three, when sexual abuse was suspected during visits with his father. I went on to talk about the different schools he attended and why. I talked about the safe house and leaving the area. Gary added many more details of Mike's behaviors over the years. The doctor needed statements from caregivers, counselors, and educators. Mike himself was to be interviewed as well as tested.

A few weeks passed before the doctor made his conclusion. He felt my son has some underlying emotional conflicts and is trying to understand who he is. In short, he can work through his problems if he continues with therapy.

I know Mike was happy about the results, but understanding why his attitude escalated from extreme highs to extreme lows was still puzzling for everyone. Two of Mike's counselors from Pathways came to our home for a visit along with some theories. They felt Mike had drug issues. This comment did not surprise Gary. I, too, was coming to the realization of the facts I could no longer deny. I began to cry.

The conversation continued with a second theory: Mike was gay.

This did not settle so easily. Instead, I insisted they were wrong, saying, "No! You don't understand. The drugs did this!"

Both counselors, along with Gary, tried numerous times to explain. I became more and more upset, yelling, "He is a boy! It's not natural! It's a personal choice! It's not right! Oh god, I can't accept this! He can change! His friends talked him into it. Oh god, no! No! No!"

Tears—lots and lots of tears—came down my cheeks. I could not handle this news. When the counselors left, Gary listened while I went on a long high-pitched flood of comments: "This can't be true! Honey, tell me this isn't true! I won't accept this! So I know other people are gay. That's their problem, not Mike's—not my son! It was Shelby's mom who brainwashed him! He's not gay!"

Gary kept insisting this was true. He also followed up with sick jokes that I did not think were funny.

Soon, I went to bed, threw my blankie on my head, and rocked back and forth, crying and repeating over and over and over all the words spoken. Morning came, but twenty minutes of sleep did not stop me from my routine at work.

Before I left, I grabbed a ball from my toy box. At work, I had another visual release for short periods of time. In the hallway or outside, I bounced the ball up and down, up and down. Some male drivers would grab it from me and toss it back. Some would bounce it hard and hit the ceiling.

I told them they could no longer play if they were not going to play by the rules. The purpose of the ball bounce was every time it hit the floor, it represented words coming at me—hard. When I caught it, this represented holding on to those words, the ones that replayed over and over. Tossing it down represented releasing those words. Hard, hold, release, hard, hold, release repetitive motion. Even though letting go of words and phrases of others is still very difficult (even today), the ball gives me an external release in a positive way.

As time went on, I used the ball as a visual to express how communication can work. I bounce the ball on the floor toward another person. They, in turn, bounce it on the floor toward me. Back and forth, words and comments work much in the same way. A person talks to another (or bounces thoughts toward another). They, in turn, wait for a response (or the return of the ball). When the ball hits the floor, it is a solid transition from one place to the next.

What is not a solid transition was the word *gay*. The world as I understood it worked off of opposites, visual logic, and order.

The next day, I saw Garth's bus pull into the garage after the morning run. I ran over to him and asked, "Is a person gay or is it nurtured?" He asked, "Is this about your son?" "Yes," I said.

Garth went on to say, "Susie, addiction can be fixed; the other cannot. They can't help it."

I was not happy about his statements. I also knew Garth had never misled me with his words, but accepting them would prove to be difficult. In the meantime, I asked many other drivers the same general question. To my surprise, more of them felt it was natural. I asked David, and he felt it was a personal choice. I was no closer to an answer than before.

However, my son's happiness kept me going in a positive way. I continued to bounce my ball, roll Silly Putty, use my yo-yo, walk on lines, fold and tear paper, snuggle my blanket, play music, attend church, and learn from the children. All these things helped take some of the edge off the internal stress.

Very soon, my son would be returning home. This transition was mixed. I liked the idea of his return but hated everything else.

CHAPTER 16

SUSIE'S RELATIONSHIP WITH THE CHILDREN ON HER BUS

Chapter 16 describes Susie's relationship with the children on her bus. Susie relates very well to the children on her bus as she has lived the life that they are living now. She understands what it feels like to be afraid of the unknown, to be forced into a position in life where they no longer feel safe.

This chapter shows us the relationship of nurturing that Susie is able to provide. She gives a safe haven to these children, with her natural instinct of love and security of those around her.

Because Susie relates better to a child than an adult, she is able to communicate more effectively with a child at her level, which results in more stability and security for the child. Susie fits well with the children on her bus as she learns the same way they do, which makes her feel very comfortable in their environment.

CHAPTER 16

At this time on my bus, there was a student who was facing a big transition of her own. She was twenty-one, with severe cerebral palsy, confined to a wheelchair, and no speech abilities. In a few weeks, the only routine she had known for years would be completely changed as graduation from BOCES grew closer. The school made arrangements for her to begin attending the United Cerebral Palsy Day Program.

I remember that Mr. Ike and I transported her to school, but we were not going to assist her inside. Instead, a teacher went on the bus to say "good morning," handed me some papers, then instructed us to transport her on to the new location.

Once Mr. Ike closed the door and started to drive away, this girl immediately began to cry. She put her left hand in her mouth and trembled with fear.

I understood fear very well. I also knew words would not help her. Quickly, I went over to her chair, knelt down along the side of her, took her right hand in my right hand, then placed the back of her right hand on the right side of my cheek. I know when I'm afraid I just need something safe and secure to hold on to. I understood her fears. I smiled softly and began humming Brahms's Lullaby.

Within minutes, this very frightened girl stopped crying. I waited quietly to see what she would do. She took her left hand out of her mouth. She took her right hand out of my hand then placed both her hands on my cheeks. I smiled. She smiled. A tear rolled down my cheek. She worked her right hand back into mine and sighed. For the rest of the trip, she held my hand tight. As she did, I softly hummed the melody again. This gave her security.

Another student who rode my bus was a boy, thirteen years old, with nonverbal issues. He carried a portable computer, but it was always in the case.

I did not know how to use a computer, but I did know it had a screen, much like a television. I could relate to television. I asked this boy if he watched television. He looked out the window. I thought about the many different TV shows I have seen over the years, including cartoons. Now I thought only of all the cartoons I have enjoyed then the jingles that went with each one. I began quietly to sing the words to the *Flintstones, Scooby Doo, Felix the Cat, Yogi Bear, Road Runner*, and many, many more.

I found myself so absorbed in the songs, and to my surprise, this boy was singing along with me. It was a connection that continued throughout the years he rode. I introduced not only jingles or songs but clips from different scenes, like "If you're not a bunny rabbit, then how come you have long ears?" The boy would talk the words along with me, and then we would both laugh.

In time, I started calling this boy "Forrest Gump." He truly liked this name. He smiled every time I said it to him. He must have seen the movie before because he knew many of the story lines in it, like "Mama always said, 'Life was like a box of chocolate—you never know what you're gonna get,'" "I gotta find Bubba!" "What is your sole purpose in this man's army?—To do whatever you tell me to, drill sergeant!" and still another, "Jenny and me were like peas and carrots."

This was Forrest's most favorite part of our play together, probably because after, we were together like peas and carrots. I would say, "Peanut Butter and Jelly," "Sauerkraut and Wiener." He would smile real big and start laughing uncontrollably after I would say that. Forrest's grandmother, father, mother and teacher gave praise. They liked seeing this boy smiling, eager to learn, and talking. I do not understand why they fussed so much. All I did was repeat what I heard.

Well, there is another student that comes to mind. She was about twenty years old, red straw-like textured hair, protruding teeth, slightly overweight, mismatched clothes, and pretty brown eyes. She was nonverbal, or at least, that is what I was told.

What she really needed was someone to take the time to listen to her at her speed. Her voice was lower than a whisper, and slow.

I had bought bows and barrettes, a new comb and mirror for her. She smiled when I introduced them to her. I asked her if she wanted to comb her hair. She smiled again. I handed her the new comb and watched as she struggled to try. I smiled and asked, "Would you like me to comb your hair?" She smiled again. I began to comb her hair and told her how pretty she was. She smiled bigger and bigger. Soon she spoke a little clearer and louder. She said, "Pretty." I said, "I know." I placed the barrettes in her hair then handed her the mirror. Her eyes sparkled as she stared at her reflection. She spoke again, saying, "I'm pretty." This girl enjoyed these special one-on-one treatments. She even shared a few short phrases of words with me. Yes, the children certainly were a joy, mostly because they were on my level of play or understanding.

Another child comes to my memory. This boy was fourteen years old when I first started this bus run, and he has since graduated from BOCES when he turned twenty-one. Anyway, he was always clowning around with Mr. Ike through the use of words. When they would see a reckless driver in another car that was pulled over by the police, the boy would yell from the back of the bus, "Hey, Mr. Ike? You think maybe that guy needs his headlights knocked out. He's a half-wit." The two of them would laugh, and the other students would join in.

This boy was one of the first students on the bus in the morning and the last off in the afternoon; so sometimes, when I would sit with him, he would mess up my hair on purpose. I would look at him and say, "Why did you just give me a bad hair day?" The boy would laugh and then say, "'Cause it's fun." He would call out to his buddy, Mr. Ike, "Susie's a psycho." So I was officially given the name Psycho Susie. We had a lot of fun until we heard that this boy had suffered a stroke-like condition and was now in a wheelchair. His right arm and leg no longer worked well; his speech was slow and slurred. It was difficult his first day back, but I did not want my concerns to cripple him more.

That night, after my chores were done, I went through all my toys in my toy box, my craft room, and bags, looking for something to lift his spirits. I found three puppets. The next day I brought them on the bus. One was of Barney (the purple dinosaur). One was of a girl, and one was a dog.

Well, I must say I did not know what voice or conversation to use for the dinosaur or the girl puppet, so I picked the dog. After the boy was secured in the wheelchair hook-ups, I took out the dog puppet, placed it on my hand, then went to him and started making panting noises and barking sounds. This made the boy laugh. Then I pressed the dog's nose, which made a squeaking sound. The boy said, "Susie!" I said, "Let me put this on your hand and see if you can start working your hand."

I placed it on his weak hand, and the boy slowly made the dog move his mouth. I told him, "You can practice moving his mouth, but no kissing." He immediately started laughing.

I told him he could take it home with him and kiss Mommy. After a few short weeks of working the puppet, he gained back most of his strength, and his spirits were high.

He still doesn't have full use of his right leg and is now in an electric wheelchair. I will miss him on the bus, but I miss all the children who have since graduated. I do plan on visiting him at his home from time to time, or calling him on the telephone just to hear him call me "Psycho Susie."

Another student I keep in touch with since her graduation is Smurf. Mr. Ike and I gave her this name early due to her size. She is about four feet tall and weights sixty-seven pounds, but she sure has a lot of personality. Mr. Ike would say, "I'll pay you fifty cents if you would come over to my house and clean my cat boxes." Smurf would say "You clean your own cat boxes!" She would slug him on his right shoulder as she boarded or exited the bus. Mr. Ike would say, "What did you slug me for?" She, in turn, would respond, "Behave! Be nice to me and Susie!"

Anyway, I learned a great deal from watching the two of them playfully socializing together. Smurf and I go on outings from time to time, keeping those old and new memories ongoing in conversations.

The student I must share in my stories is the one I can relate to the most. He was fifteen years old at the time he rode on our bus and very autistic, to the point that he has retreated into an infantlike state. When he first came into our routine, he was in a stroller. Now the staff at the school did not want him to use this anymore. Instead, he was to use the stairs and sit in a seat, like the rest of the children who were not in wheelchairs.

With the first afternoon of this transition, it was easy to see what was happening with him as I watched. As the children boarded the bus one at a time, his fears began to surface; he began rocking, then curling into a fetal position by raising his legs up along the back of the seat in front of him. He began to put his left hand in his mouth.

I gently placed the palm of my right hand on his forearm, pushing his hand away from his mouth. I placed the palm of my hand on his knees, pushing his legs gently back to the floor, softly speaking the word no. I knew he would begin biting himself if his fears escalated, just as I did so many years ago. I understood fears very well and knew what was happening with him.

As each child entered the bus, he heard different tones of voices, different words of communication, and he even saw quick glimpses of facial expressions. This created a rapid increase of anxiety for him, resulting in an overload of his senses he could not process. He only knew how to react impulsively, retreating into an old behavior. This boy only wanted to stop the scrambling inside. He did not know any other way. As the noise elevated, I reminded the children to use their inside voices.

I also had my duties of unloading the wheelchair for students upon arriving at their homes. When I went to the back of the bus to do this, the boy would lay on his back in a half-fetal position; put his hand in his mouth; bite down; put his feet up, kicking the window, screaming; and a flood of tears poured out of his eyes. When I returned to his seat, I had to take the palms of my hands on his legs, push, and swing them back to the floor and work at sitting him back up.

All this time, I whispered very softly, "Shhh—it's okay to be afraid. It's not okay to hurt yourself." Repeating over and over and over softly, "Shh—it's okay to be afraid. It's not okay to hurt yourself." The boy soon stopped crying, placed his fingers of his left hand in between the fingers of my right hand, and then leaned on my left shoulder, calm and quiet for the rest of the trip. He only wanted to feel safe and secure but was not able to relay this into words. When my fears begin to surface words become difficult to process. I have learned to channel this energy much more appropriately and have found that I can accept guidance from others, especially if the voice of another is soft and soothing.

CHAPTER 17

SUSIE'S COLLEGE EXPERIENCE

Chapter 17 describes Susie's graduation from high school, which led to her experience in college. Two weeks before Susie's high school graduation, her English teacher took her aside and asked her why she would not complete her reading homework. Soon, he discovered that Susie was about to graduate from high school and yet was not able to read.

Susie graduated as planned and went on to college, where she worked with JoAnn, an OVR counselor. During this time, JoAnn learned that Susie was not able to read but was pushed through high school based on being told what to do and then doing it. Susie also followed this same practice in college. She was able to do the work if told to do it, so reading was not a necessity for her.

Even though Susie was able to perform academically and achieve high grades, socially she was an outcast, which led to her dropping out of college. Susie wasn't able to interact with the other college students. They would ask her questions and try to get her to socialize, but she would become scared and cower away. This resulted in her physically losing weight and passing out on one occasion to where the doctor pulled her out of college. Susie's college days came to an end.

CHAPTER 17

With all this discussion about students, graduations, teaching, and behaviors, it has prompted specific memories of my difficult times in school. Two weeks before my high school years ended, my English teacher, Mr. Wilson (who taught sports and literature) approached me after class. He requested that I stay as he wanted to talk to me about a concern he had.

I sat in my seat in the front row. He sat on his desk with his arms folded across his chest. He said, "Susie, I need you to explain something to me." His tone of voice was stern and frightening to me, so I looked down at the floor for a few moments.

He said, "You come to my class every day and are not a problem. You sit quietly and listen to the discussions in class. You are not a problem in the school. My question to you is, How come you never turn in your homework after I give you your reading assignments?"

I remember sitting in my seat staring at the door, unable to speak a word; but the more serious his tone of voice became, the more tears would build up in my eyes.

Mr. Wilson changed his position and was now standing, raising his arms in the air, insisting that in order to pass his course, the reading assignments were necessary. He walked back and forth past me, going on to say, "Susan, I just don't get what the problem is! It is not like you can't read!"

After he spoke those words, I began to cry out loud. He did not know that without a picture, I could not comprehend the words on the pages of the books.

Mr. Wilson sat back on his desk, but his tone was much different, quieter, and softer. He said, "You can't read, can you?"

I was still unable to speak a word, but I was shaking uncontrollably. Mr. Wilson leaned over toward me then said, "You are going to graduate in two weeks, and you can't read. How did this happen?"

I did receive my diploma on time, but I did not feel it was right to give me something I did not earn. Some years after high school was over, I was sent to the Office of Vocational Rehabilitation (now known as VESID). This was arranged by the psychiatric outpatient treatment assigned to me. They said I qualified for their services.

My counselor at OVR, JoAnn, wanted me to try schooling at a local community college. There were many issues that developed during this new transition. One was after I took tests to establish where my academic skills were, the school staff discovered a disturbing fact. This was that I only had a third-grade reading and math level.

My counselor at OVR called me into her office to discuss this matter. JoAnn said, "Susan, I thought you said you graduated from high school?"

I said, "I did. You made a copy of my diploma."

She said, "Oh, that's right—but how come you only have a third-grade reading and math level?"

I could only repeat my experiences from so long ago. I told her my parents took me out of a Catholic school after the end of my third year and then put me in a public school. The fourth grade teacher, Mrs. Johnson, kept insisting that because of the change of schools my academics suffered; however, she felt that I would catch up.

At the end of fourth grade, I had nineteen unsatisfactory marks on my report card, along with twelve Ds, or below-average marks, mostly in the subjects of math, spelling, and reading.

Of course, my third-grade year was basically the same as the fourth grade. I struggled with reading, math, and spelling, and worked better independently or one-on-one. I went on to tell JoAnn that fifth and sixth grades were much the same—more problems with reading, math, spelling, and taking in new information.

JoAnn kept looking at me as if I were making this up. I said, "I can give you my old report cards to look at if you would like to see for yourself."

She said, "No, that's alright. I believe you. I just cannot understand why the education department never caught this problem in the first place.

"Anyway, Susan, I wondered something."

I said, "What?"

She sat in her chair with her left elbow on the chair arm and her fingertips touching her head just above her left ear, then flipped her hand towards me as she spoke. "If you only have a third-grade math level, then how come you did so well in the four years of drafting you took in high school—especially since this is what we are aiming for in college?"

Well, I began a long story of explaining. "JoAnn," I said, "it was like this. For the four years I was in drafting class, I was the only girl. I did not know anything about problem solving or, for that matter, percentages, fractions, ratios, decimals; and of course, I still struggle with multiplication and division.

"What I did know was to follow simple directions. When Mr. Bird, our teacher, asked if anyone needed help, I was quick to go to his desk to get assistance. I told him I needed a visual in order for me to understand what it was that he wanted.

"So, Mr. Bird would sketch a rough draft of the object to be drawn. He would say, 'Okay, take this home, clean it up, and put the dimensions on it. Oh, and make sure you use good line quality and lettering.'

"I, in turn, would do what he requested then turn it in the next day. Mr. Bird would look it over, decide it was good, and give me a 90, 95, 97, 99, or 100 grade on it. So, you see, I only did what I was told."

JoAnn sat in her chair with her right elbow on her desk and her right hand holding her chin, moving her head back and forth. I said, "What? What's the matter? I told you the truth!" She just kept repeating the word *amazing*.

We continued to discuss the upcoming college semester. JoAnn concluded that a change in the courses was necessary. Reading and math were mandatory if I was to succeed, and so they were scheduled: the independent reading and an independent basic math course.

The reading was very difficult. There was no pictures or graphs to relate any visual. I worked hard but only advanced to a fifth-grade level.

The basic math course was scary, but the book I received had plenty of charts, graphs, pictures, and big numbers. I did very well to the point I advanced into the regular classroom to learn algebra, geometry and trigonometry. The teacher was patient with all the students in the class as she would go over and over the same formulas on the chalkboard. In time, I advanced to above average in my mathematical skills.

I added another course later. This was machine tools. Half the class was lecture; the other half, shop. The lecture part was easy because I could watch the movies, filmstrips, or listen to the teacher as many times as I needed in order to complete the workbook. If I had time before my next class or before the bus came, I went to this lecture classroom again and again in order to understand. I did well once again, averaging in the 90s.

The other half of this course was the shop.

The very first day, when the entire class showed up, the teacher walked all of the students through the machine shop, stopping at each machine to show us how each one worked. Fifteen minutes before class ended, the teacher directed all the other students (all males) except me to go back through the shop with his teaching assistant and review the tour. I was asked to stay behind.

The teacher handed me the metal object that he had assembled throughout the tour. He said, "Susan—it is Susan, isn't it?"

I said, "Yes, sir."

He said, "You're here through the OVR program aren't you?"

I said, "Yes, sir, that is correct."

He said, "Take this with you and do not come back to this class until the last day of class."

I said, "But, sir—"

He insisted, "No more discussion. Just do what I told you and bring it back with you on the last day of the semester."

I was uncomfortable with his request, yet he escorted me out of the door by walking behind me. He kept saying, "Just bring it back on the last day of the semester."

My fears created a deep puzzling of scrambled thoughts. Every time I tried to explain the experience to JoAnn, it came out something like this: My tone was high pitched and squeaky, my breaths short and panting, and the words came out "... and he told me, but I didn't know what to do." This anxiety was followed up with tears.

Her comments were, "Susan, you misunderstood his intentions," or, "Susan, what are you trying to say? I don't understand you." Still, JoAnn would insist, "Susan just go back to school and keep doing what you are doing. You're doing well for yourself."

So I did return to the class at the end of the semester, as requested, with the metal object in my hand. The teacher looked it over and gave me a 96 on this project—a grade I did not deserve.

As I continued my education in college, other fears mounted inside. These were the social interactions. People always wanted to know what I was going to school for or asking me if I was married, if I had a boyfriend, what music I liked, did I like sports. I thought, what does any of this have to do with going to college? One small group of boys was heard to say, "She is pretty, but she is slow. She must be stupid." Then their laughter followed.

As a result of all this scrambling and fears, my body was restless; my appetite decreased; and on one occasion, I passed out. My doctor pulled me out of this environment, and my college days were over.

What I have come to realize about myself throughout many of my experiences over the years is that I must learn at a much slower speed in order to comprehend and reduce anxiety. Words can lose me in conversation with no visual expression. So I do fit in well with the children on my bus because many of them learn in the same way.

CHAPTER 18

SUSIE'S LIFE WILL ALWAYS BE A LEARNING EXPERIENCE

Chapter 18 describes how Susie's life will always be one of learning in the world in which she lives. Because of her autism, she will always learn the best with rules, routine, and orders. She will always continue to rely on her ball, Silly Putty, tearing papers, playing her harp, walking on lines, or spinning her yo-yo. To you and me, these may sound like odd behaviors; but to Susie, they are a way to keep her life in order and in balance.

She will always live a simple life. However, because of those around her, the simplicity of life could become very complex in a blink of an eye; and when that occurs, she will turn to one of her toys to put her life back in balance.

CHAPTER 18

My son is much more challenging for me to connect with because he learns quickly, does not always need visual guides, and has a social interest more advanced than I do. He never did get a diploma; however, he earned his GED. He has a job and lives away from home. I may not always like what he does in his life, but I'm sure he can succeed if he chooses. In the meantime, I continue to work on my own issues: making better eye contact, trying hard not to repeat words or phrases or talk in great lengths about a particular subject.

I continue to bounce my ball, roll Silly Putty, tear paper, play my harp, walk on lines, or spin my yo-yo when anxiety increases. Many obvious signs of autism have been suppressed, although I do remain very regimented with rules, routine, and order. I still have my security blanket and will always need some guidance or direction from others. I continue to work at the bus garage. Funny thing about that—transitions have always been painfully difficult, yet transporting these special needs students has educated me along the way.

I know my life will never be simple. I will always struggle with a need to have answers to why situations happen as they do. Social stories from trusting people are a must during those difficult times. New words or phrases without a picture to follow can also spiral my anxiety out of control. Internal comfort for me has been a lifelong problem, but my experiences (although very challenging) have pushed me into a new understanding of the world outside of autism. I also am much more aware of understanding myself.

I would certainly *not* recommend that others on the autistic spectrum follow my footsteps. I have been most fortunate to have had a remarkable network of supportive individuals who gave positive directions throughout my journeys.

My dad once said, "Susan, you are going to have to adjust to change in order to survive." I am much more confident, productive, and independent than ever before. I dedicate this to all those folks who saw my potentials.

INDEX

Edwards Brothers,Inc!
Thorofare, NJ 08086
30 June, 2010
BA2010181